DIV
ERS
ITY,
INC.

DIV ERS ITY, INC.

THE FAILED PROMISE *of a* BILLION-DOLLAR BUSINESS

PAMELA NEWKIRK

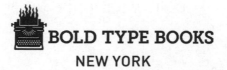

BOLD TYPE BOOKS

NEW YORK

Bold Type Books
116 East 16th Street, 8th Floor New York, NY 10003
www.boldtypebooks.org
@BoldTypeBooks

Printed in the United States of America

First Edition: October 2019

Published by Bold Type Books, an imprint of Perseus Books, LLC, a subsidiary of Hachette Book Group, Inc. Bold Type Books is a co-publishing venture of the Type Media Center and Perseus Books.

The Hachette Speakers Bureau provides a wide range of authors for speaking events. To find out more, go to www.hachettespeakersbureau.com or call (866) 376-6591.

The publisher is not responsible for websites (or their content) that are not owned by the publisher.

Print book interior design by Amnet Systems.

Library of Congress Control Number: 2019941714
ISBNs: 978-1-56858-822-3 (hardcover), 978-1-56858-823-0 (e-book)

LSC-C

10 9 8 7 6 5 4 3 2 1

To Marjani and Mykel

CONTENTS

PREFACE

I have devoted a considerable portion of my life to journalism and higher education, both fields in which people of color are radically underrepresented. In three of four newsrooms, I was the only African American news reporter. I would later become one of two people of color on New York University's tenure-track journalism faculty and for a time was one of the few tenured African American female professors on the entire faculty of the university's Faculty of Arts and Science.

During more than three decades of my professional life, diversity has been a national preoccupation. Yet despite decades of handwringing, costly initiatives, and uncomfortable conversations, progress in most elite American institutions has been negligible. While racial/ethnic minorities make up roughly 38.8 percent of the national population, they comprise just 17 percent of full-time university professors, which includes faculty at Historically Black Colleges and Universities (HBCUs).[1] Put another way, non-Hispanic Whites, who comprise roughly 61 percent of the population, hold 82 percent of full-time professorships. Hispanics and Blacks, who together encompass roughly 31 percent of the US population, are just 3 percent and 4 percent, respectively, of full-time professors.[2] Their numbers have barely budged over the past few decades.[3]

The field of journalism has not fared much better. Four decades after the newspaper industry pledged to create newsrooms that reflect the proportion of minorities in the population by the year 2000, they, too, remain disproportionately White. African Americans, Latinos, Asians, and Native Americans combined held 16.55 percent of newsroom jobs, based on the 2017 annual newsroom survey released by the American Society of News Editors.[4] That number was even a slight decrease from the preceding year, and when online news sites were excluded, the percentage of minorities dropped to 16.3 percent.

The numbers in journalism and academia, like those in other influential fields—from the arts, advertising, and fashion to law, technology, and investment banking—defy the quickening pace of change in the nation's racial demographics. In 2011, for the first time in America's nearly 250-year history, more babies of color were born than non-Hispanic Whites. Since 2010, non-Hispanic Whites have been the minority in twenty-two of the nation's one hundred largest metropolitan areas, and the US Census Bureau projects that by 2045 they will no longer constitute a national majority—which has made diversity one of the buzzwords of the twenty-first century. But why, after five decades of countless studies, public pledges, and high-profile initiatives, is diversity lagging in most elite fields? And why do many White Americans believe that racial progress has been much better than the numbers suggest?

Our current diversity conversation began in 1968, when President Lyndon Johnson's National Advisory Commission on Civil Disorders recommended the inclusion of African Americans in institutions that had historically excluded them. The Kerner Commission, as it came to be known, highlighted the need to address the shameful legacy of slavery and Jim Crow. It overlooked, however, the haunting invisibility of Native Americans, an estimated 90 percent of whom were killed by disease and war in the wake of European settlement. Native Americans and Alaskan Natives, including those of more than one race, number around 6.7 million, or 2 percent of the population.[5] Regrettably, given their small numbers, they barely register in much of the data.

Since 1968, diversity, of course, has been expanded to encompass other racial and ethnic minorities along with women, people with physical and mental disabilities, LGBTQIA individuals, and other marginalized populations. However, given the issues unique to each distinct group and the ways in which the plight of racial minorities in general and African Americans in particular have been overshadowed by other categories within this overtaxed term, this book will specifically address the progress the nation has made toward *racial* diversity.

Race, of course, is a complicated and often-imprecise designation that in the United States has always relied less on ancestry than on appearance. Those who most resemble what is considered White are generally accorded greater status. It's a messy social construction that nonetheless matters when trying to sense the texture of American life for distinct segments of the population. But it is challenging, given the shifting terrain. The classification of Hispanic/Latinx connotes ethnicity and not race, which could range from Black to White. And given the invisibility of Native Americans in most metrics and the ascendance of Asians in STEM fields and in income earning, there is no way to paint a complete portrait of America's complex racial landscape. Further clouding the picture, Asians—who encompass a broad spectrum of people, cultures, and languages across a continent—are, relative to their numbers in the general population, either disproportionately over- or underrepresented, depending on the field.

To examine the nation's progress toward racial diversity, I focus on the three largest racial/ethnic minority groups: Hispanics/Latinx, African Americans/Black, and Asian Americans. I alternately use African American or Black and Hispanic for the sake of clarity, even though the terminology in the data I cite varies. Encompassed within race and ethnicity are, of course, all the other classifications—including physical and cognitive disability, gender, and sexual orientation—that become doubly or triply burdened by interlocking systems of discrimination. Still, a half century after Kerner, the Black-White divide is still most palpable in American life; the stark disparities between the two groups remain the most telling indicators of America's racial breach. However, the expansion of America's racial tableau and the long history of discriminatory federal policies and attitudes directed at other Americans considered non-White require an examination of efforts to fold racial and ethnic minorities into the mainframe of the nation. America, despite the presence and contributions of many, remains—at least in the public imagination and in most realms of influence—dominated by Whiteness.

I explore diversity across numerous fields but pay sustained attention to three fields in particular: academia, Hollywood, and corporate America—each of which has publicly and privately grappled with the issue over the past five decades. They are among the fields whose leaders have in recent years renewed their commitment to diversity, collectively pledging billions of dollars to commission studies, set up training sessions, and hire consultants and czars to oversee diversity programs. These efforts have, among other things, shored up a multibillion-dollar industry, expanding opportunities for an ever-growing number of law firms, consultants, and senior-level executives. It's impossible to understand diversity without exploring the big business of it, the tension between the rhetoric and expenditures, and the chronically disappointing results. In recent years, organizations have begun to use the term *diversity and inclusion* to underscore the need for compositional diversity *and* institutional belonging. Unless otherwise indicated, the word *diversity* will imply both.

In examining the data and conversing with scores of people on the front line of the movement for change, I discovered some of the reasons why, despite decades of deliberation and multibillion-dollar initiatives, many are still pondering and gesturing rather than meaningfully increasing diversity. Perhaps most surprising is that many of the fields that are considered the most progressive, such as the arts and entertainment, are the least diverse and that corporate America—despite remaining challenges—has in many instances made far greater strides toward employing and promoting racial minorities.

The plodding pace of change a half century later makes clear the need to reframe the diversity conversation of recent years from a rosy we-are-the-world ideal to one fired by a mission to combat systemic racial injustice and pervasive delusion about where we stand. Our current predicament is part and parcel of an enduring ideology of White preeminence and the callous resolve that America's global ascent justified the means by which African Americans, Native Americans, and others were ruthlessly exploited. This ethos permeates mass media, so-called high art, the Western literary canon, and our criminal justice and educational systems. The dismal numbers reported year after year are a predictable outcome of this morally impoverished calculus. Unless and until White America—including those who claim progressive values—comes to terms with its complicity in persisting injustice, diversity initiatives will continually fail. Since one's complicity can be willful or stem from benign ignorance and neglect, the latter affords the potential—if not the promise—of serious reflection and reform. The numbers are uninspiring, but the all-too-few examples of change offer a semblance of hope. They can serve as a beacon for those who are truly committed to justice. In the end, we will each be judged not by stated principles but by our achievements.

Given the sturdy foundation of White domination on which America rests, it has perhaps been naïve of many diversity advocates to expect even those viewed as progressive allies to relinquish hardwired attitudes and centuries-old customs, no matter how ignobly attained. Many believed that if only they could show the inherent injustice of institutional bias and the ways in which it perpetuates inequality and fuels racial conflict, then attitudes—and workplaces—would substantially change. Five decades later, diversity proponents can be forgiven their idealism, if not their fidelity to ineffective approaches.

Allies and advocates of diversity—including those who are beneficiaries of the burgeoning industry it has spawned—must also change course lest they become complicit with those who consciously or unconsciously work to sustain the status quo. In their work they might ask whether they unwittingly serve as smokescreens rather than true agents of change. How might they enable evasion and resistance by the institutions they serve? At what point does it become apparent that institutions they associate with are less committed to diversity than their rhetoric, commissioned task forces, studies, and appointed diversity officers suggest?

How do we as a society gauge success, and at what point is it safe to assume that some of the best efforts are in vain? And what can be done differently to foster change?

Diversity, Inc. inspires indelicate questions and sober reflection. In an increasingly multiracial nation, who will set the course for the nation's identity and destiny? In a nation that has—as a result of political and numerical dominance—largely been defined by Whiteness, what would a truly diverse society mean culturally, politically, spiritually, economically, and psychologically for White Americans? What would it mean for America?

1

DIVERSITY AND DISCONTENT

"Race prejudice has shaped our history decisively;
it now threatens to affect our future."
—Report of the National Advisory Commission on
Civil Disorders, 1968

Clarence Otis Jr. was nine years old when in 1965 an upris-ing in his Watts neighborhood helped the embers of unrest that for the rest of the 1960s swept through Black urban America. Nearly five decades later, Otis—who in 2004 became one of the nation's seven Black Fortune 500 CEOs when he was tapped to lead Darden Restaurants—credits the aftermath of that upheaval for his future success.

In 1967, Johnson, in response to the spiraling turmoil, empan-eled the National Advisory Commission of Civil Disor-ders, which, a year later, in a blistering report, largely blamed White racism and indifference for the despair plaguing African

Americans. A century after emancipation, it called on leaders of American institutions to address "pervasive discrimination in employment, education and housing which has resulted in the continuing exclusion of great numbers of Negroes from the benefit of economic progress."[1] The report cast in stark relief White America's systematic exclusion of Blacks from decent housing and education and positions in trades and professions, including news media, Hollywood, and corporate America.

Johnson had already laid out his ambitious vision for a more racially just and inclusive nation in the early months of his presidency. In a 1964 speech at the University of Michigan, Johnson said that a Great Society "rests on abundance and liberty for all. It demands an end to poverty and racial injustice." In a nation flush with prosperity, some thirty-six million Americans, nearly three-quarters of whom were children and senior citizens, were living below the poverty line.

He quickly ushered in sweeping legislation, including the Civil Rights Act of 1964, to outlaw discrimination in public accommodations and federally funded facilities, and the Voting Rights Act of 1965, which forbade literacy tests and other measures that had prevented southern Blacks from voting. The 1965 Higher Education Act made work study, federal grants, and low-interest loans for college making it more accessible to the poor and working class. Medicare, Medicaid, food stamps, and the 1966 Child Nutrition Act brought health care and greater food security to the poor and elderly. Jobs Corps established skills training and temporary employment; and Head Start, as its name implied, offered early education along with medical and dental care to level the playing field for poor children.

Johnson moved quickly to enforce the new laws targeting injustice. He substantially increased federal funding for hospitals and schools, then used those funds as a lever to ensure compliance with Title VI of the Civil Rights Act forbidding discrimination based on race, color, or religion in public accommodations and facilities that received federal funding. He dispatched inspectors to schools and hospitals across the South to monitor compliance.

As Joshua Zeitz, author of *Building the Great Society*, said, the results were "astonishing."

Between 1965 and 1968, he said the number of Black students in the South who attended better-resourced majority-White schools rose from roughly 2.3 percent to almost 23.4 percent and peaked at 43.5 percent in 1988. Between 1968 and 1980, the portion of southern Black children attending schools where they made up more than 90 percent of the student population declined from 77.5 percent to 26.5 percent.

Moreover, by 1964, just 26 percent of Blacks attained a high school diploma, but within a decade the percentage had increased to 41 percent. By 2017, 87 percent of Blacks age twenty-five and older had attained a high school diploma, nearly closing the gap with Whites, whose rate stood at 93 percent.[2] While similar numbers are not available for other racial groups during the early years of the Civil Rights Movement, between 1964 and 1984, the gap between Blacks and Whites closed from 24 points to 16 points.

Hospitals, nursing homes, and other facilities that received federal funding were also desegregated under the watchful eye of inspectors. Facilities found out of compliance were ineligible to accept Medicare and Medicaid, which became law in 1965.

Following passage of the Voting Rights Act, federal examiners swept into Alabama, Louisiana, Mississippi, and Georgia, where by the following January some ninety thousand voters were added to the rolls. By 1970, about 66 percent of African Americans in the Deep South were registered, and most were able to vote.

While the Civil Rights Movement turned the spotlight on southern bigotry, the urban riots highlighted the persistence of northern discrimination that kept Blacks in overcrowded, under-resourced neighborhoods and excluded them from most professions and unions. By the end of the 1960s, many doors that had long been closed to urban Blacks were suddenly pried open.

"We were beneficiaries of the Great Society," said Otis, one of four children reared by a janitor and homemaker. Otis and his siblings took advantage of programs such as the Neighborhood Youth Corp, a federally funded program that created jobs for urban teens, and the Watts Town Arts Center, which brought recreation and culture to his segregated and economically fragile neighborhood.

"We got a head start," Otis said. "It definitely mattered during that era."[3]

Otis graduated among the top one hundred of seven hundred students in Los Angeles's predominantly Black David Starr Jordan High School, most of whom attended college—in his case the prestigious Williams College, from which he graduated magna cum laude. He went on to Stanford Law School and by age thirty was a vice president at First Boston Corporation. In 1995, he was recruited to Darden—the restaurant group that included Red Lobster and Olive Garden. He continued to move up the ladder, becoming chairman and CEO nine years later. Under his leadership, share prices nearly tripled, and Darden, with 185,000 employees and two thousand outlets, ranked as the largest full-service restaurant operation in the world.[4] During the last four years of his tenure, *Fortune* magazine listed Darden as one of the top companies to work for.

Otis assembled a senior leadership team that was 41 percent of color. "When you have these kind of senior leadership numbers it becomes easier to make diversity a priority in everything you do—from hiring and talent management (development and promotion) to culture building to how you think about and treat customers," he said.[5]

But in recent years diversity in many American industries has stalled and in some instances is in retreat. Otis stepped down in 2014, and with the retirement in 2018 of Kenneth Chenault as CEO of American Express, the number of Black Fortune 500 CEOs has decreased to three. African Americans, who comprise roughly 13 percent of the US population, are fewer than 1 percent of Fortune 500 CEOs. Just under 4.5 percent of Fortune 500 CEOs are Black, Hispanic, or Asian. People of color hold about 16 percent of Fortune 500 board seats.[6]

"The fact that we're in this situation is, I think, a real problem and embarrassing for corporate America," Chenault said before stepping down.[7] "One of the biggest issues for our society is diversity and inclusion. We should have far more representation."

The numbers are telling. Between 2009 and 2018, the percentage of Black law partners has inched up from 1.7 to 1.8 percent. People of color comprise 9 percent of law firm partners, compared to 71 percent who are White male, and 20 percent women, according to the National Association for Law Placement.

Between 1985 and 2016, the proportion of Black men in management at all US companies with one hundred or more employees barely budged, from 3 percent to 3.2 percent.[8]

So a half century after Johnson's clarion call for African American inclusion in the mainstream of American life, they and other racial minorities remain strikingly underrepresented in most elite fields, particularly in management. While Johnson's programs and policies have begun to bear fruit, he may have underestimated the depth of White resistance to full racial equality. While northern Whites had supported civil rights legislation aimed at the South, they resisted efforts to integrate schools and housing closer to home. In 1966, legislation barring discrimination in the sale and rental of housing sparked a vehement backlash and ultimately failed. That year, Rev. Martin Luther King Jr., who had been felled by a rock during a demonstration in Chicago, remarked, "I think the people of Mississippi ought to come to Chicago to learn how to hate."[9]

Johnson's transformative vision became a target for conservative politicians from Ronald Reagan to Paul Ryan, who worked tirelessly to dismantle key programs and policies that had begun to disrupt generational poverty and had created long-denied opportunity for African Americans and other disadvantaged groups for a quality education and gainful employment.

In *White Rage*, historian Carol Anderson recounts how Black unemployment had sharply declined during the 1960s and 1970s, nearly closing the racial gap. However, under the Reagan administration, federal jobs and programs that had aided that progress were cut, causing Black unemployment to skyrocket to 15.5 percent—the highest it had been since the Great Depression. Black youth employment rose to 45.7 percent.

"At this point Reagan chose to slash the training, employment and labor services budget by 70 percent—a cut of $3.895 billion," Anderson wrote, causing college enrollment among African Americans to tumble from 34 to 26 percent.

"Thus, just at the moment when the post-industrial economy made an undergraduate degree more important than ever, 15,000 fewer African Americans were in college during the early 1980s than had been the case in the mid 1970s," she wrote.[10]

Today, many school districts are as segregated as they were in the 1950s when *Brown v. Board of Education* deemed segregated schools unconstitutional. Millions of Black and Brown children are condemned to overcrowded, under-resourced schools in neighborhoods that Great Society programs were attempting, with demonstrable success, to address.

Reaganesque ideology has helped fuel a never-ending series of legal challenges of any measures intended to create opportunity that laws and racial custom has historically denied Blacks and now other non-Whites.

The recurring obstruction of Black advancement dates back to the Reconstruction era when measures to make amends for centuries of slavery were met with racial terrorism and Black Codes, a series of laws passed in southern states that for another century blatantly denied Blacks their constitutional rights. Today, any attempt at racial redress is predictably met with legal challenges. The examples are numerous and, by now, expected. Legions of Whites, from Allan Bakke in 1978 to Abigail Fisher in 2013 and 2016, have made the claim of reverse discrimination to undermine policies that aim to create opportunities for those who, by design, were historically left out. In 2019, Mark Perry, a White economics professor at the University of Michigan, filed a complaint with the Department of Education Office for Civil Rights against Wayne State University for hosting a summer workshop for the not-for-profit group Black Girls Code. The organization seeks to address the acute underrepresentation of Black women in the burgeoning tech industry. Perry had reportedly filed more than thirty similar complaints challenging gender discrimination across the country. However, his latest effort threatened to undercut efforts to expand opportunity for one of society's most economically disadvantaged groups.

The sluggish pace of change has in recent years sparked claims of institutional soul-searching and a renewed commitment to diversity. In 2017, a group of global CEOs launched CEO Action for Diversity and Inclusion; more than five hundred business leaders publicly pledged to advance diversity and inclusion in the workplace. In 2018, the law firm Shearman & Sterling was among the prestigious global outfits to hire its first-ever chief diversity officer and establish a task force to increase diversity.

The Ford Foundation is betting the farm on its ability to help diversify American institutions, throwing the full weight of its more than half-billion dollars in annual grants toward initiatives that promote equality. "Progress won't come without us being uncomfortable," Darren Walker, the foundation president, said. "People want to believe we can have diversity and not really get uncomfortable . . . It requires incumbent leaders and managers to change their behavior and practices. It means that institutions have to change incentive structures and to fundamentally interrogate their own behavior, which is very uncomfortable."[11]

But therein lies the problem. There's little evidence that many are inclined to accept that challenge. Leaders in numerous fields have for decades stated their commitment to diversity, but recent employment data invite scrutiny of their efforts. Especially revealing is the significant underrepresentation of people of color in some of the fields often touted among the most progressive, including the arts, journalism, academia, fashion, and the film industry. As Walker said, much of the answer lies in overcoming the sense that racial inequality and discrimination have been overcome. "The challenge in the progressive community is benign neglect; benign validation," states Walker. "When you look behind the curtain, the emperor has no clothes."[12]

In 2015, an art museum demographic survey commissioned by the Andrew W. Mellon Foundation found that 84 percent of museum curator, conservator, educator, and leadership positions were held by non-Hispanic Whites, with 6 percent Asian, 4 percent African American, 3 percent Hispanic White, and 3 percent two or more races. Racial minorities were most often employed as museum security guards. "The case is clear and urgent," Mariët Westermann, vice president of the Mellon Foundation, wrote in the report's introduction. "Constructive responses to it will be critical to the continued vitality of art museums as public resources for a democratic society."[13] However, that same year, Samantha Niemann, a White student denied a Getty Foundation internship created to address the dearth of racial minorities in museums, filed a lawsuit charging discrimination. A 2018 Mellon survey indicated the numbers of people of color in leadership remained small.

Sixteen years after installation artist Fred Wilson was awarded the MacArthur Fellowship, known as the "Genius Grant," for work highlighting biased museum practices, art world professionals in 2015 formed the Museums and Race organization "to challenge and reimagine institutional policies and systems that perpetuate oppression in museums."[14] The group seeks to address the lack of diversity on museum boards and staffs and among its collections, members, and visitors.

At every turn, purportedly liberal and elite sectors maintain racial custom and tradition in their hiring until they are publicly shamed or otherwise coerced into widening access to people of color. In New York City, Mayor Bill de Blasio made waves when he announced that the city would use city funding as a hammer to pressure cultural organizations to diversify their overwhelmingly White boards. In New York City, where the population is 32 percent White, its cultural workforce is nearly double that, with leadership decidedly Whiter. The city also pledged $1 million to subsidize diversity programs at its cultural institutions. Similar efforts are under way in cities across the country.

In 2019, two iconic fashion world labels—Gucci and Prada—announced the creation of diversity initiatives after an outcry over designs that resembled blackface. Both fashion houses pulled the items from the shelves, and Prada quickly established a Diversity and Inclusion Advisory Council for which as its public face it enlisted two prominent African Americans, artist-activist Theaster Gates and director Ava DuVernay. Gucci hired a global diversity czar and vowed to create multicultural scholarship and a more diverse workforce. That same season, Burberry also came under fire for a runway design that featured a hoodie and what appeared to critics to be a noose. In a statement, the fashion house expressed regret for its insensitivity. "We will reflect on this, learn from it and put in place all necessary actions to ensure it doesn't happen again," read a statement by Marco Gobbetti, the company CEO.[15]

Not surprisingly, like other exclusive sectors, racial and ethnic minorities are virtually excluded from top management and
corporate boards in fashion. A 2018 survey of the fifteen largest
public fashion and apparel companies found that only 11 percent of board seats were held by non-Whites, and 73 percent of
chief executives were White men.[16]

The newspaper industry, which for decades has vowed to
diversify its professional ranks, also came under scrutiny when
in 2016 Liz Spayd, the public editor for the *New York Times*,
faulted the paper for "preaching" but not practicing diversity.[17]
Spayd noted that only two of the more than twenty reporters
assigned to the 2016 presidential campaign were African American and none were Latino or Asian. Moreover, all six White
House reporters were White, while the Metro staff had only
three Latinos among its forty-two reporters in a city with
the nation's second-largest Hispanic population. The entire
Style section writing staff was White, and none of the paper's
twenty-one sports reporters were African American, "yet blacks
are plentiful among the teams they cover."

Spayd pointed out that the only non-White on the masthead
was Dean Baquet, who in 2014 became the first African American to serve as executive editor in the paper's 163-year history.[18]
Baquet, who had served as editor of the *Los Angeles Times*, is also
among a handful of African Americans who has ever helmed
an American daily newspaper. At daily newspaper and online
outlets that responded to the survey, Whites hold 83.4 percent
of newsroom jobs and are 86.6 percent of newsroom leaders.
The American Society of News Editors' annual survey does not
indicate what percentage of editors helming news organizations
are people of color, but the number has always been miniscule.[19]

The discomforting critique did not win the already embattled Spayd many friends at the *Times*, and in July 2017 the paper disbanded its public editor role, calling it outdated. Perhaps it is, but Spayd's critique was not: while African Americans held 9 percent of *New York Times* newsroom jobs in 2015, in 2018 their percentage had slightly dipped to 8 percent.[20] There was a slight uptick for Asians from 11 percent to 12 percent, Hispanics from 5 to 6 percent, and multiracial from 2 to 3 percent, respectively.[21] That said, the *Times* is far more diverse than most American newspapers. Four decades after the newspaper industry pledged to have newsrooms that reflect the proportion of minorities in the population by the year 2000, they remain disproportionately White. In the face of declining newspaper circulation and industry belt-tightening since the early 2000s, the field's commitment to diversity has receded. In fact, the number of minorities in newsrooms declined between 2002 and 2015.[22] During that time, the number and percentage of Black journalists reported in the ASNE survey fell from 2,951 journalists (5.23 percent) to 1,560 (4.7 percent). There were also 721 fewer Hispanic journalists, who held 1,377 (4.2 percent) of newsroom jobs, and 357 fewer Asian journalists, whose numbers stood at 926 (2.8 percent).[23]

In September 2018, the American Society of News Editors (ASNE), which since 1978 has released annual newsroom demographic surveys, postponed releasing the survey results due to historically low participation. Only 14 percent of the seventeen hundred newsrooms responded, compared to nearly 40 percent the preceding year, an indication that diversity may not be a foremost concern. The previous year, ASNE was awarded a $300,000 grant to create a more comprehensive diversity survey, but it apparently did little to inspire participation.

The 2019 survey was expanded to include LGBTQ journalists. ASNE has now set a goal of doubling the number of minorities—by 2025.

Meanwhile, some of the nation's most prominent magazines have long operated under the radar as they are not included in annual demographic surveys. They, too, have historically maintained disproportionately White editorial staffs.

Elsewhere in the journalism industry, the numbers are similarly bleak. In radio, people of color hold just 11 percent of newsroom jobs and are nearly 6 percent of news directors. While the numbers in television broadcasting have long exceeded those in radio and print, people of color, despite gains, remain disproportionately underrepresented. The 2018 survey of TV and radio newsrooms by the Radio Television Digital News Association found the TV news workforce at non-Hispanic stations is 21.4 percent people of color at network affiliates and 22.7 percent overall, the greatest amount of representation ever. But it falls far short of parity. While the population of people of color rose 12.4 percent since 1990, their numbers increased 7 percent in the television workforce.

What's more, their numbers dwindle at the top. Just 6.4 percent of general managers were of color, down 1 percent from 1995. Even at Spanish-language stations where the staff is predominantly Hispanic, 36.4 percent of general managers were non-Hispanic White. People of color hold just 14.3 percent of news director jobs at non-Spanish-language stations.

In 2019, *CBS News* caused a Twitter storm when it released its slate of twelve digital reporters and associate producers assigned to the 2020 presidential campaign. While the team included four people of color, none were African American, the nation's largest racial minority. The omission was especially conspicuous at a time when Blacks are disproportionately affected by a number of high-profile national issues, including overpolicing and mass incarceration, gun control, voter suppression, and widening income and education disparities. Among the critics was Alexandria Ocasio-Cortez, the newly installed member of the House of Representatives from New York who tweeted: "Unacceptable in 2019. Try again." Sarah Glover, president of the National Association of Black Journalists, said it's unfortunate diversity remains a problem more than fifty years after the Kerner Commission Report. "CBS's political team takes previously heralded steps back half a century," she said.[24]

Hollywood also attracted unwanted attention over revelations that for two years in a row none of the Academy Award acting nominees were of color, prompting #OscarsSoWhite—a campaign launched by nascent activist April Reign—to go viral on Twitter. A *Los Angeles Times* study in 2012 found that in the then eighty-three years since its founding, the academy voters were overwhelming White and male and that fewer than 4 percent of the Oscar awards for acting had been given to non-Whites.[25] Four years later, Stacy Smith, the coauthor of a University of Southern California study, concluded that "there's not just a diversity problem in Hollywood; there's actually an inclusion crisis."[26]

If the tech industry portends the future, then the forecast at Google, LinkedIn, Facebook, and the other Silicon Valley tech giants is uninspiring. At Facebook, African Americans comprised 1 percent of technical and 2 percent of leadership roles, according to Facebook's *2018 Diversity Report*. Three percent of Hispanics were in technical roles, and their numbers in leadership roles dropped from 4 percent to 3 percent. Eighty-three percent of Silicon Valley executives are White, and mostly male. In 2016, Black and Latino candidates at Google each made up 4 percent of all new hires. Google's overall workforce is 54 percent White, 40 percent Asian, 4 percent two or more races, 6 percent Hispanic or Latinx, 3 percent Black, and less than 1 percent American Indian or Alaskan Native and Native Hawaiian or Pacific Islander. Meanwhile, roughly 26 percent of bachelor's degrees in science, technology, engineering, and mathematics (STEM) fields were conferred to Blacks and Hispanics, according to the National Center for Education Statistics.[27] Blacks, Hispanics, and Native Americans earned about 18 percent of bachelor's degrees in computer science, and between 2015 and 2016, Blacks and Hispanics were 10 percent and 12 percent, respectively, of computer science majors.[28]

In 2018, in the wake of its fifth "disappointing" diversity report, Facebook appointed former American Express CEO Kenneth Chenault as its first African American board member. Chenault was also added to the board of Airbnb, the tech hospitality company, in the wake of widespread reports of racial discrimination by hosts. Other tech companies, including Apple and Uber, have begun releasing their own diversity reports.

The severe underrepresentation of Blacks, Hispanics, and women in tech has fueled tension and headlines. In 2017, a memo by a White male employee denigrating Google's diversity efforts created a national firestorm, culminating in his firing.[29] In 2015, Twitter—already under fire for its glaring underrepresentation of Blacks (2 percent) and Latinos (4 percent)—triggered a backlash when it hired Jeffrey Siminoff, a White male, to fill a job as vice president for diversity that had been held by a woman.[30] Siminoff had been the diversity chief at Apple, where he was succeeded by

Denise Young Smith, an African American woman who stepped down after months on the job amid controversy over comments she made that some believed devalued diversity.

Renewed calls for diversity are playing out against the backdrop of resurgent White nationalism. A half century after Johnson's appeal for racial inclusion, an American president has openly spurned diversity as an American ideal. Prior to his election, Donald Trump for years implausibly questioned the citizenship of America's first African American president and denigrated Mexicans, Muslims, and urban Blacks. Trump's Executive Order 13769 entitled "Protecting the Nation from Foreign Terrorist Entry into the United States," known as a Muslim travel ban, inscribed Islamophobia into federal policy. The widely condemned executive order was ultimately struck down by the courts and significantly diluted, but draconian immigration policies ensued.

To stem the tide of migration largely by people seeking asylum from Central and Latin America, the Trump administration began separating parents from their children and interring them in cages. Trump also came under fire for describing himself as a "nationalist"—which was viewed as a dog whistle to White nationalists—in the wake of his administration's mishandling of relief efforts after Hurricane Maria in Puerto Rico claimed an estimated three thousand lives and for allegedly calling African nations "shithole countries" and asking why the United States wasn't taking more immigrants from places like Norway.[31] In 2018, Trump posted on Twitter: "A vote for Democrats in November is a vote to let MS-13 [the Mara Salvatruca gang] run wild in our communities, to let drugs pour into our cities and to take jobs and benefits away from hardworking Americans."[32]

In 2018, the FBI reported that hate crimes had spiked 17 percent over the previous year, the third consecutive year of a reported increase.

Meanwhile, a wave of protests at college campuses—including some of the nation's most prestigious and progressive schools—has illustrated the extent to which racial tensions persist over many of the same issues that roiled campuses in the 1960s. Among the colleges and universities under fire were Yale, Princeton, Oberlin, and Wesleyan, where students complained about the racial climate, the paucity of faculty and students of color, and the curriculum. Figures from the National Center for Education Statistics suggest why: during the fall of 2016, among full-time professors at degree-granting postsecondary schools, 82 percent were White (55 percent male; 27 percent female), 10 percent were Asian/Pacific Islander, 4 percent were Black, 3 percent were Hispanic, and 1 percent or less were two or more races or American Indian/Alaska Native. And as previously indicated, these figures include faculty at Historically Black Colleges and Universities.[33]

The quest for racial diversity has long been an uphill crusade, but it's now waged in a far more polarized climate in which many Whites now claim that they are being disenfranchised as others are afforded undue advantage. An NPR poll conducted in 2017 found that 55 percent of White Americans believe they are discriminated against, while, tellingly, a lower percentage said they had actually experienced discrimination.[34] A Reuters survey in 2017 found that 39 percent of Whites polled agreed with the statement that "White people are currently under attack in this country."[35]

Many Whites saw the presidential election of Barack Obama as evidence that racism is passé and African Americans have achieved equality—if not unmerited advantages. The *New York Times* optimistically proclaimed, "Obama Elected President as Racial Barriers Fall" despite polling data that showed that in 2008 Obama received just 43 percent of White votes compared to 95 percent of Black, 67 percent of Hispanic, and 62 percent of Asian votes.[36] In 2012, Obama received 93 percent of Black, 73 percent of Asian, and 71 percent of Hispanic votes. The percentage of White voters dropped to 39 percent. Both times he lost the White vote, with White women divided and White men decidedly opposed.

Nonetheless, the term "post-race" became ubiquitous, while "political correctness" or "PC"—the valuing of sensibilities that fall outside of the White, Christian, heterosexual mainstream—became a slur. White men—who retain dominance over every influential field—increasingly claim that they, and not those who by law and custom had historically been shut out, are under siege.

Today, it is not uncommon to hear even those who are considered White progressives complain of White male discrimination, despite their overwhelming overrepresentation in most American institutions. Few take the time to consider that the centuries-long dominance of White males was only possible due to the subjugation of women and people of color—a legalized oppression rationalized by baseless inferiority theories rooted in religion and the academy. Sadly, these beliefs continue to resonate, and some view their domination as a birthright and racial minorities who seek parity as unentitled trespassers.

Whether heralding a post-race era or lamenting that they were losing ground, many Whites conveniently ignored the harsh reality of a widening economic chasm between Blacks and

Whites. Between 1983 and 2013, the wealth of the median Black household declined 75 percent (from $6,800 to $1,700), and 50 percent for Latinos (from $4,000 to $2,000), while wealth of the median White household rose 14 percent from $102,000 to $116,800. The median income for Blacks was 65 percent of that of Whites, up only slightly from 59 percent in 1970. In 2018, the poverty rate for Whites was 8.4 percent, compared to 21 percent for Blacks, 18 percent for Hispanics, and 10 percent for Asians.[37] Black unemployment has consistently been at least twice as high as it is for Whites for most of the past five decades.

Even as some bemoan the decline of White men in the workplace, the extent to which their numbers have dropped is primarily due to the progress of White women. Since 1968, when President Johnson expanded affirmative action policies to include women, White women have made far greater strides in professions and in college admissions than have people of color.[38] For example, while between 2004 and 2018 the percentage of White men on Fortune 100 boards declined from 71 percent to 63 percent, the largest gain was experienced by White women, who hold 221 board seats—or 18.4 percent. That compares to a mere 29 seats held by African American women, 11 by Latina women, and 17 by Asian women. Overall, between 2004 and 2016, the White composition of board seats had changed little—decreasing from 85.2 percent to 82.5 percent. During that time, White men lost fifty-one seats and White women gained twenty-eight. All other racial groups had single-digit increases of five or fewer seats, except for Latino men, who lost two seats. To be sure, *all* women—White women included—remain disproportionately underrepresented, with women of color barely represented at all. But between 1985 and 2014, the proportion of Black men in management barely budged (from 3 percent to 3.3 percent), compared to White women, whose proportion increased from 22 percent to 29 percent.[39]

Still, the idea that racial barriers have fallen has swayed court decisions. Among the most glaring examples is the 2013 US Supreme Court's five-to-four vote striking down key provisions of the 1965 Voting Rights Act that for decades had protected African Americans from blatant acts of voter disfranchisement.

"Our country has changed," Chief Justice John G. Roberts Jr. wrote in his unduly optimistic majority opinion. "While any racial discrimination in voting is too much, Congress must ensure that the legislation it passes to remedy that problem speaks to current conditions."

In doing so, the court patently ignored current conditions and the continuing barriers to African Americans' voting rights and those of other marginalized populations. Since that decision, more than twenty-two states passed restrictive statutes making it harder to vote. In 2017, the United States Court of Appeals found that North Carolina's voting restrictions had specifically targeted African American voters "with almost surgical precision."[40] The Supreme Court moved to rule as unconstitutional two of the state's gerrymandered congressional districts.

When viewed as a zero-sum game, it is perhaps understandable that those who historically had all the marbles fear that equal opportunity will mean they'll have fewer. From that reductive vantage point, even those who see themselves as progressive adherents of American ideals might privately—and sometimes publicly—view diversity as a threat. Even as they retain a disproportionate share of the pie, many Whites apparently fear that, in this land of plenty, gains for racial minorities will imperil them.

That fear might explain why exit polls indicate at least 62 percent of White males and some 52 percent of White females voted for Trump despite his political inexperience, multiple bankruptcies, erratic temperament, and racially and sexually offensive rhetoric that would ordinarily preclude one from assuming the US presidency.

Anxiety over immigration and the nation's shifting racial demographics overshadows critical economic problems afflicting Americans of all races. Between 1980 and 2014, income growth increased 616 percent for the top 1 percent, 194 percent for the top 10 percent, and only 4 percent for the bottom 20 percent.[41] Between 1970 and 2016, the income gap between Americans at the top and the bottom increased 27 percent.

Compounding growing inequality is the rise in automation and the fact that many Americans of all races are ill prepared for jobs that would go unfilled if not for immigration. The same day that Trump scapegoated immigrants in a 2018 speech in Montana, a report from ADP and Moody's Analytics warned that the nation's labor shortage had reached a critical shortfall. It cited figures from the Bureau of Labor Statistics that showed that, for the first time, there were more openings than available labor.[42]

In addition, climate change threatens to cause the loss of 1.2 billion jobs in fields like agriculture, fisheries, and forestry and a 30 percent drop in the GDP by the year 2100 unless the nations that most contribute to the rise in carbon gas intervene.[43] The state of Maine has already seen a decline of lobsters off its coast. Into this void of imagination, leadership, and progressive policies enter demagogues who prey on centuries-old fears to sow division, while growing income inequality across all races, and the abundant opportunities that are needlessly squandered, go ignored. Rather than post-race, the nation is becoming post-White, and race appears to matter more than ever.

However, while the evidence is all around us, too few acknowledge the effect of racial bigotry or the resistance to racial inclusion in fields in which people of color have historically been left out. In New York City, where I often attend events that blend the arts, publishing, academia, and journalism, I'm often struck by the racial homogeneity I find in these presumably progressive settings. This was never more striking than during a dinner I attended at a school in New York. Following a lecture by a noted White chronicler of the Civil Rights Movement, the conveners, led by the school president, assembled for a private dinner of roughly seventy-five people, virtually all of them White. The scene, replete with mostly Black uniformed servers lining the room, could have been one from the 1950s South the author had earlier recounted. But this was 2018 New York City, and the irony had been lost on my fellow table guests.

So diversity—or more pointedly the paucity of it—is a vexing issue that cuts across political persuasions; even some of the paragons of progressivism often fail to notice the elephant in these monochromatic rooms. Like an endless loop, these segregated settings reproduce workplaces that reflect homogenous social spheres.

CHAPTER

2

THROUGH THE LOOKING GLASS

"The price of culture is a lie."
—W. E. B. Du Bois, *The Souls of Black Folk*, 1903

On January 15, 2015, at a little before 8:00 a.m., April Reign retreated to her family room to watch the live televised announcement of the Academy Award nominations. Reign had spent the preceding weeks viewing films with many of the likely contenders and eagerly sat before her flat-screen TV for the disclosure of the closely guarded list of nominees. Reign's anticipation soon faded to incredulity and disappointment as White actor after White actor were named for the acting categories. Among the actors overlooked were those who starred in *Selma*, the critically acclaimed civil rights drama nominated for Best Picture and directed by Ava DuVernay, one of Hollywood's few African American female directors.

Reign, then aged forty-four and an avid Twitter user with nearly eight thousand followers, logged on to express her frustration before heading to her Washington, DC, office where she practiced campaign finance law. By lunchtime, to her astonishment, her hashtag #OscarsSoWhite was trending internationally on Twitter, sparking a global conversation about the lack of diversity in Hollywood.

"It was just one tweet," Reign said. "There was nothing deep."

Until then Reign had little connection to the film industry other than as an ardent movie-goer. Her hashtag made her a coveted guest on panels and at film festivals and the subject of countless media interviews. "I needed to get up to speed and do a lot of reading."

Reign began devouring articles to figure out what kind of roles people of color had been nominated for or won over the past eight decades. She also dug into who had been overlooked for the Academy Awards or even cast in Oscar-worthy roles.

"Now I talk to networks about diversity and inclusion issues," Reign said. "They bring me in to say we have this show, what do you think about the name, the premise, the cast. I have screenwriters send me their scripts. I've become this voice for diversity and inclusion," work that Reign now pursues full time.

In the aftermath of the firestorm, the Academy moved to diversify the ranks of its then 5,765 voting members, who a *Los Angeles Times* study found were 94 percent White and 77 percent male, with a median age of sixty-two. The composition helped explain why, over the course of eighty years, only 4 percent of Oscars had been bestowed on Black actors.

Hollywood has a long and shameful history of racial stereotyping and exclusion. Since the inception of film, African

Americans, Latinos, Asians, and Native Americans have been depicted in often demeaning and one-dimensional ways. During the silent film era, Black characters were typically presented as lazy and shiftless or as a buffoonish punchline. Characters in films like *Rastus in Zululand* (1910), based on a lazy odd-job man who is captured by African cannibals, were perpetuated in many popular films. *Rastus in Zululand* inspired a string of sequels, including *Rastus' Riotous Ride* (1914). According to a synopsis in *Moving Picture World*, the era's influential film industry journal, the film is based on the wedding of Rastus's only daughter, which it called "a big social event in Coonville."[1]

In many of the early films, as on stage, Black characters were played by White actors in blackface. In addition to the Rastus sequels, which featured multiple White actors, White actors in blackface appeared in such films as *Uncle Tom's Cabin* (1903) and *The Birth of a Nation* (1915).

Racial stereotyping was not limited to African Americans. Five years before *The Birth of a Nation* was released, Asians were demeaned in D. W. Griffith's film short *That Chink at Golden Gulch* (1910). Like blackface, yellowface predates film and began with minstrelsy on stage.

Meanwhile, the 1929 film *Hearts in Dixie* broke ground by featuring an all-Black cast; even then, the actors were confined to stereotypes. That film included Stepin Fetchit, who as an African American actor helped legitimize the trifling, shuffling Black character in film. Fox Film Corporation's *Hearts in Dixie* was followed by MGM director King Vidor's *Hallelujah* (1929), which also portrayed Blacks as childlike and buffoonish. The stock Black characters were later expanded to include the Mammy, a trope that was canonized in 1940 when Hattie

McDaniel became the first African American awarded an Oscar. She won for her supporting role as the stereotypical Mammy in the epic Civil War drama *Gone with the Wind* (1939). The film won a total of ten Academy Awards, including Best Picture, Best Director, and Best Actress.

The 1915 film *The Birth of a Nation*, based on a book that romanticized slavery and Ku Klux Klan violence, triggered a virulent backlash from Blacks, with picketing outside theaters and protests by the NAACP. Activist journalists Ida B. Wells and Monroe Trotter were among those seeking a ban or the censorship of the film's most egregious parts on the grounds that it instigated violence against Blacks. They met with President Woodrow Wilson to seek his support, but he instead screened the film at the White House and hailed it as one that was "like writing history with lightning." The film went on to become one of the most successful and beloved films in Hollywood history.

This same period ushered in the establishment of independent film companies, largely bankrolled by White studios and operated by Black filmmakers, such as Oscar Micheaux, to create films targeted to African Americans. The first all-Black cowboy film, *Harlem on the Prairie*, was released in 1937. Numerous films with all–African American casts, including *Cabin in the Sky* (1943) and *Stormy Weather* (1943), were released during and after World War II, making stars of performers such as Lena Horne, Ethel Waters, and Butterfly McQueen.

In 1937, the Negro Actors Guild was founded in New York City to assist Black performers. One of the cofounders was the actress Fredi Washington, who became one of the era's most vocal critics of the limited opportunity and recognition of African American actors. Other founding members included

W. C. Handy, Paul Robeson, Ethel Waters, and Bill "Bojangles" Robinson, who served as honorary president. While its primary role was to provide financial assistance to entertainers, it would also align itself with other groups committed to civil rights.

Washington had starred on Broadway and then appeared in a string of films, most notably the original 1934 version of the Oscar-nominated film *Imitation of Life*. Her stirring performance would win her acclaim, but she was routinely overlooked for other roles, in part due to the Motion Picture Production Code, called the Hays Code, which explicitly prohibited the depiction of miscegenation in film. Washington, with her green eyes and light tan skin, did not fit the stereotypical role of a maid and was viewed as too light for all-Black films. Her skin was darkened for her costarring role with Bill Robinson in *One Mile from Heaven* (1937), after which she became more vocal as an activist.

In the 1940s and 1950s, Washington actively participated in the Cultural Division of the National Negro Congress and the Committee for the Negro in the Arts, two organizations committed to racial equality and the eradication of racial stereotypes in the arts.

Washington publicly castigated Academy Award–winning producer Louis de Rochemont and director Alfred Werker for casting White actors to play middle-class Black characters in the film *Lost Boundaries* (1949), a film based on a true account of Scott Carter, a light-skinned African American physician who eventually passes for White after he's unable to get work as an African American. The film won the Cannes Film Festival award for best screenplay.

In a letter to the *Los Angeles Daily News*, Washington challenged Werker's claim that he didn't cast African American actors in the film because "the majority of Negro actors are of the Uncle Tom, Minstrel show, shuffling dancer type of performer." Washington said she was "appalled and not a little fighting mad" over his remarks.[2] "There are many Negro actors and actresses who are consistently turned down for plays and screen fare on the excuse that they are too fair, too intelligent, too modern looking, etc., I know, because I am one who falls into this category."[3]

Noting how she had in *Imitation of Life* played the role of a "neurotic, sensitive, fair Negro girl," she asked, "but did Alfred Werker give me an interview for either of the two female roles in *Boundaries*? He did not. He simply was not interested in learning what he evidently did not know; that there are many legitimate Negro actors and actresses who are far more intelligent than Werker proves himself to be."[4]

She'd later divulge how, early in her career, she had been advised by studio executives to pass for White in order to move into the Hollywood elite. Years later, Raquel Welch, born Jo-Raquel Tejada, had blended into the White mainstream by assuming her husband's last name and appearing to play down her Bolivian ancestry. She became one of the era's biggest film icons and sex symbols but later said she felt she had lost part of her identity. However, she successfully fought to keep her first name, which studio handlers thought was too ethnic.[5] Washington, however, was uncompromising. "Frankly, I do not ascribe to the stupid theory of White supremacy and try to hide the fact that I am a Negro for economic or any other reasons. If I do I would be agreeing that being a Negro makes me inferior."[6]

Exacerbating the problem for actors of color prior to the 1950s were segregated theaters in which Blacks were restricted or relegated to the least desirable seats. In 1946, Swedish actress Ingrid Bergman petitioned the Actors Equity Association to take a stand on the issue. That year she was scheduled to perform at George Washington University's Lister Auditorium, where, a week earlier, African American members of the American Veterans Committee—an interracial group of World War II veterans—were denied admission.

While she filled her contractual commitment to perform in *Joan of Lorraine*, she along with playwright Maxwell Anderson and fellow members of the all-White cast petitioned for an Actors Equity ruling forbidding members to participate in future productions in Washington, DC, theaters. The ruling was backed by the Dramatists Guild of America, which included most of the country's leading playwrights. In 1947 the Lister Theater lifted its ban, but the National Theatre continued to restrict Blacks. Actors Equity resolved that no actors belonging to the association would perform in the National Theatre in Washington until it lifted its ban.[7]

Meanwhile, in 1953, the Coordinating Council for Negro Performers, along with the Negro Actors Guild, released a survey that found that one-half of 1 percent of performers shown in a single week on any of television's four stations was Black. "The absence of Negroes in any but an occasional menial role gives a distorted picture of one-tenth of the nation's population, which in turn prejudices the struggle of the Negro for full citizenship," the survey stated. "So the point at issue is more than just jobs for Negro actors, but one of the principal forces that can help or hinder the drive toward the realization of full democracy."[8]

A statement issued by the Actors Equity Association, the Dramatists Guild of America, and the League of New York

Theaters and Producers called on "all responsible elements in the allied entertainment arts" to work toward "the integration of Negro and other non-Caucasian artists in all media of the performing arts."[9]

Decades later, similar findings provoke the same calls for racial inclusion that quickly fade from the headlines until the next commissioned study unfailingly draws the same disappointing conclusions.

In 1959, Samuel Goldwyn's $7 million motion picture production of *Porgy and Bess*—a so-called African American opera with music and lyrics by George Gershwin—was promoted as a cinematic breakthrough. The glitzy, highly anticipated film followed a Broadway version that had opened in 1935 to rave reviews. Directed by Otto Preminger, the film starred Sidney Poitier as the crippled beggar Porgy and Dorothy Dandridge as the drug-addicted Bess. The film flopped at the box office—grossing half of what it cost to make—and received mixed reviews. It ultimately was awarded a Golden Globe for Best Picture and a Best Actor and Actress nominations for Dandridge and Poitier. The film also received four Academy Award nominations for cinematography, costume, sound, and musical score, and won for costume design. It also received a Grammy Award for best soundtrack.

Following the film, Dandridge—a singer and ravishing beauty—struggled to find work in film. This was despite her Oscar-nominated performance as Best Actress in *Carmen Jones* (1954). While Hollywood had few roles for a talented caramel-toned woman, she was able to find nightclub work and was the first African American to headline at New York City's Waldorf Astoria hotel. She would do two films in Europe before her final film *Murder Men* (1961), in which she played a drug-addicted singer. The role appeared to mirror struggles in her own life. She died in 1965 at age forty-two. The Los Angeles medical examiner determined the probable cause of death was an overdose on antidepressants.

Meanwhile in 1964, Sidney Poitier—who had initially feared taking the stereotypical role of Porgy—went on to become the first African American to win an Oscar for Best Actor for his lead role in *Lilies of the Field*, a film in which he plays a handyman who comes to the aid of nuns who seek to build a chapel in the desert.

"It has been a long journey to this moment," Poitier said upon accepting his award.

It would take another four decades before a Black woman received an Oscar for Best Actress, when Halle Berry won for *Monster's Ball* (2001). (Fifteen years later, Berry said she was "profoundly hurt" that her breakthrough did not lead to greater opportunity for other people of color.)[10]

Poitier would go on to star in other films, including *A Patch of Blue* (1965) in which he plays an office worker who helps a blind White woman who falls in love with him. While a box office hit, a scene in which the woman kisses Poitier's character was cut in the version shown in the South. Elizabeth Hartman, who played the blind woman, was nominated for an Oscar. In *Guess Who's Coming to Dinner* (1967), Poitier's character addresses a taboo subject—a Black man engaged to a White woman. The critically acclaimed film grossed $56.7 million and garnered Oscars for costar Katharine Hepburn and Best Screenplay. The film was also nominated for Best Actor (Spencer Tracy), Best Picture, Editing, Best Director, and Best Supporting Actress (Beah Richards). Poitier was the only central actor overlooked.

For African Americans, the 1970s would mark a Hollywood renaissance as a multitude of films featuring casts and story lines catered to a Black audience. The so-called Blaxploitation era would create opportunities for Black directors, actors, and crews largely deprived of work and an audience that craved representation. Films like *Blackenstein* (1973) and *Blacula* (1972) satirized popular White horror films, whereas others—like *Three the Hard Way* (1974) and *Shaft* (1971) depicted African Americans as heroic avengers of White supremacy and criminality. But many of the films mined the same well of stereotypes that leaders such as W. E. B. Du Bois had decried in the 1920s. The 1970s brought to the screen a parade of gangstas, pimps, drug dealers, and prostitutes. But the genre enabled African Americans to break into producing and directing. Among those leading the pack were Gordon Parks: *Shaft* (1971), *Superfly* (1972), and *Three the Hard Way* (1974); and Melvin Van Peebles: *Sweet Sweetback's Baadasssss Song* (1971). Actors Sidney Poitier and Ossie Davis also made their directorial debuts with *Buck and the Preacher* (1972) and *Cotton Comes to Harlem* (1970), respectively. The popular genre made household names of actors like Pam Grier, Fred Williamson, and Richard Roundtree, who throughout the 1970s remained fixtures in films that satiated an African American audience while demonstrating the viability of the Black market.

Then in 1991, filmmaker Julie Dash became the first African American woman to release a feature film with her critically acclaimed *Daughters of the Dust*, a visually arresting period film that explored Gullah culture at the turn of the century. Like other Black filmmakers, she had to overcome a wall of rejection before she was able to release her iconic film.

On television, Black middle-class respectability, epitomized by *The Cosby Show* (1984–1992), harkened back to groundbreaking shows like *I Spy* (1965–1968), also starring Bill Cosby, and *Julia* (1968–1971), the first network show starring an African American woman in a non-stereotypical role. The show, an instant hit, starred Diahann Carroll, who won the Golden Globe award for Best Female TV Star for her role depicting a middle-class nurse. Like *The Cosby Show*, which featured an upscale African American family helmed by a doctor and a lawyer who lived in an elegant brownstone, both shows faced criticism for not depicting *authentic* Black life, as if middle-class Black families were unrealistic. (On *The Cosby Show*, the characters reveled in Black culture and achievement.)

Carroll found the criticism hurtful, and she often met with civil rights leaders to try to ameliorate concerns. "I cannot spend every weekend studying each word, writing an analysis of everything I think may possibly be insulting, then presenting it to you in the hope that we might come to an understanding," she told show creator Hal Kanter.[11] By the end of the third season, the pressure proved too great, and she asked to be released from her contract.

Nearly two decades later, *The Cosby Show*, which had been turned down by ABC before it was acquired by NBC, became the highest-rated series on network television. It led to the popular spinoff *A Different World* (1987–1993), which was based on the experiences of students attending a Historically Black College.

Susan Fales-Hill was among the writers of color who rode the wave of the Cosby franchise. "It's a nepotistic industry. I was there in part through nepotism," said Fales-Hill, whose mother, Josephine Premice, was a star of the Broadway stage who later appeared on television shows, including *The Jeffersons* (1975–1985) and *The Cosby Show*.[12] Fales-Hill was a senior at Harvard College when her mother, over dinner, regaled Cosby with stories about her daughter who wrote French tragedies in French. Her mother called Fales-Hill to tell her Cosby wanted to meet her. "I wrote up a spoof of *Lifestyles of the Rich and Famous* and did an audio cassette and sent it to him. He thought it was hilarious. He said, 'I want to get you in this business. You need to be in this business when you graduate.'"

Cosby set up an interview for her at *Saturday Night Live*, where she said she got the "polite brush-off. They had zero interest. He said, 'Never mind. You'll be an apprentice on *The Cosby Show*.'"

Upon graduating, Fales-Hill flew out to Los Angeles to join the *Cosby* writing team, most of whom had experience in stand-up comedy or theater. "Basically for the first month I showed up every day and would sit in the cubicle and no one would talk to me," she said. "I had skipped a lot of levels. They were actually right. 'Is she a princess or is she serious?'"

Over time, her persistence paid off and she became a writer. At the time, Matt Robinson was the lone African American writer. Thad Mumford, an African American television pioneer, would come in to write guest scripts.

After two years at *Cosby*, Fales-Hill was offered an opportunity to become a story editor for *A Different World*, which doubled her salary and gave her an onscreen credit.

Mumford was the producer of the show for which Fales-Hill would become known as the voice of Whitley, a southern belle played by actress Jasmine Guy. The character had been inspired by one of the show's writers who had gone to college with a similar character.

Slightly more than half of the crew was of color who, along with women, assumed powerful positions. "It was nirvana," Fales-Hill said. In the second year, Debbie Allen, the African American choreographer and actress, was brought in as a producer. Allen would take the crew on a pilgrimage to Historically Black Colleges each year to conduct research. Fales-Hill credits Allen for using the show as a forum for issues that students were experiencing on college campuses.

"It was very powerful—an amazing and unique environment. It was Bill [Cosby]'s insistence, and Tom [Werner] and Marcy [Carsey] were committed to it," she said of the Carsey-Werner production team. By the third year of the show, Fales-Hill had become a head writer.

The success of *The Cosby Show* and *A Different World* did not inspire imitation. In 1999, the NAACP threatened to boycott and sue ABC, CBS, NBC, and FOX when none of the twenty-six shows in their fall lineup featured a single person of color in a lead role. After a series of meetings, the networks agreed to a host of diversity initiatives. Two decades later, writers of color are still a rarity in television and in film.

"You're still routed the Black way," Fales-Hill said, referring to Black-themed shows. "The crossover is hard and limited."

By the 1980s, the wave of Blaxploitation films had receded as major studios responded to the proven marketability of Black actors by releasing a spate of films starring a handful of leading men, including Eddie Murphy, who appeared in a string of big-budget crossover films. In many, he played the comedic character alongside a White actor, as he did in the blockbuster films *Trading Places* (1983) and *Beverly Hills Cop* (1984). Murphy broke the mold in *Coming to America* (1988), in which he played an African prince who sought to assimilate into African American life, a film that atypically played into the fantasies of Black viewers.

In *Coming to America*, Murphy's character is a dignified prince from a mythical African kingdom that seemed to foreshadow by three decades the fictional sub-Saharan country Wakanda in the 2018 smash hit *Black Panther*.

Tim Reid, the actor and filmmaker who during a forty-year career starred in several network shows, including *WKRP in Cincinnati* (1978–1982), *Frank's Place* (1987–1988), and *Sister, Sister* (1994–1999), believes he paid a price for promoting diversity on the *Frank's Place* set. The show, created by Hugh Wilson, chronicled the life of an African American professor at Brown University who inherits a restaurant in New Orleans, where the show was set. The critically acclaimed show often dealt with issues of race and class.

Reid believes he employed an unprecedented number of Black people behind the camera, noting the number of vice presidents, accountants, writers, and technicians he hired on the set of *Frank's Place*.

I brought back and resurrected a lot of careers. And I would catch a lot of flak for it. They said I was making a statement. It cost me a lot of unnecessary rancor but I always wanted to give people around me an opportunity. Some Black people would say, "Don't push it so hard." When I was doing it there weren't that many. You could get all the Black people in a van. You look behind the scene, even now. There's more diversity than there's ever been but there are very few people who can green-light a project.[13]

Reid, as the executive producer and star of *Frank's Place*, had reached the highest echelon of television. The show was nominated for a Golden Globe and won three Emmy awards, along with a TV Critics Association Award for Outstanding Achievement in Comedy and an NAACP Image Award for Outstanding Lead Actor in a Comedy Series. Still, it was cancelled after one season and was ranked number three on *TV Guide*'s list of sixty shows that were "Cancelled Too Soon."

"People who control the message live in the shadows, in the board room," said Reid. "Only a few have controlled the image. When we tried to do that, the battles I found myself in. It's amazing. It's like I was creating uranium. Every union, every producer, they shunned me. I was trying to tell stories that were not only untold but were purposely overlooked or hidden."

Progress for Asian and Latino actors has been similarly protracted. Like their Black counterparts in young Hollywood, Asian actors often competed for roles against White actors who appeared in yellowface. Examples include the Asian character in the 1915 film *Madam Butterfly* played by White screen star Mary Pickford. Even screen icon Katharine Hepburn played an Asian character in *Dragon Seed* (1944). One of the most prominent examples of yellowface was the depiction of a Chinese character, Charlie Chan, first by the White actor Warner Oland, in the popular series of some forty films produced by Fox (later Twentieth Century Fox) beginning in the 1930s. Also, in 1961, in *Breakfast at Tiffany's*, the legendary actor Mickey Rooney stereotypically depicted an Asian character with buckteeth and a mumbled accent.

However, beginning in the 1920s, two actors of Asian descent managed to break through the barrier. Sessue Hayakawa, the Japan-born actor, and Anna May Wong, a Chinese American actress, were cast in films that would normally use White actors in yellowface. But unlike Hayakawa, who played leading men, Wong typically appeared in supporting roles.

Born Wong Liu Tsong in Los Angeles in 1905, Wong's first major film, *Toll of the Sea* (1922), was loosely based on the opera *Madame Butterfly*. In the film, Wong played the self-sacrificing character Lotus Flower, who falls in love with a White American visiting China. The silent film, Hollywood's first shot entirely in Technicolor, was a hit. Wong was just seventeen years old.

But while the role showcased her talent and beauty, she was continually relegated to supporting roles. For Wong, like a long line of actors of color to follow, the price of inclusion was marginalization and stereotyping, their limited roles filtered through a prism of White imaginings. In *The Thief of Bagdad* (1924), starring and produced by Douglas Fairbanks, she was cast as a Mongol slave, Dragon Lady. More often than not, she lost lead roles to White actresses such as Myrna Loy. Throughout the 1920s, and before achieving fame for her role in *The Thin Man* movie and sequels, Loy played a series of Asian characters. Wong appeared with her in *The Crimson City* (1928), a film starring Loy, who again played an Asian character. Wong again lost a starring role in *The Good Earth* (1937) to Louise Rainer, the White actress who won an Oscar for Best Actress in the film for her performance as a Chinese woman. Wong also lost a part to Helen Hayes, who played a Chinese character in *The Son-Daughter* (1932). Wong was cast in a supporting role in the

Oscar-winning film *Shanghai Express* (1932) starring Marlene Dietrich.

Wong moved to Europe in 1928 to avoid typecasting in Hollywood. There, she achieved stardom. "I was so tired of the parts I had to play," she told a reporter from *Film Weekly* magazine. "Why is it that the screen Chinese is always the villain? And so crude a villain—murderous, treacherous, a snake in the grass. We are not like that. How should we be, with a civilization that is so many times older than that of the west?"[14] She returned to Hollywood in 1930, and after appearing in the hit play *On the Spot*, she starred in *Daughter of the Dragon* (1931) in the role of a quintessential Dragon Lady. The role of her father, Fu Manchu, was played by the White actor Warner Oland, who would go on to play Charlie Chan. The stereotypical roles would provoke hostility toward her by some in China. Wong, widely considered the first Asian American movie star, died in 1961 at age fifty-six.

Though Asian actors appeared in numerous films from the beginning of cinema, Ben Kingsley, whose father is Indian, became the first actor of Asian ancestry to win an Oscar for Best Actor following his 1982 lead role in *Gandhi*. Two years later, Haing S. Ngor became the third when he won a Best Supporting Actor Oscar for his role in *The Killing Fields* (1984). Not until 2006 would Ang Lee became the first Asian director to win an Oscar, for *Brokeback Mountain*. He won a second in 2013 for *Life of Pi*.

Actors of Hispanic descent have also had to navigate a field in which most non-White actors are routinely typecast.

Carmen Miranda, the Brazilian-born singer and actress, became a major star in the United States in the 1940s, but she was mostly marginalized as the scantily clad singer and dancer who donned her famous fruit-adorned hat. Miranda, a former hat maker, had designed the hat based on the traditional head-dress worn by Black female fruit merchants in Brazil.

In 1951, José Ferrer, born José Vicente Ferrer de Otero y Cin-trón in Puerto Rico, became the first Hispanic actor to win an Oscar for his role in *Cyrano de Bergerac*. He had previously won a Tony for playing the role on stage. In 1985, Ferrer also had the distinction of becoming the first actor awarded the National Medal of Arts. In 1952, the Princeton University graduate would go on to win a Tony for his role in *The Shrike* and a Best Director award for three plays, including *The Shrike*. He would direct the film version in 1955.

In 1953, Anthony Quinn, born Antonio Rodolfo Quinn Oaxaca, a native of Mexico, became the second Hispanic actor to win an Oscar when he was awarded Best Supporting Actor for his depiction of Mexican revolutionary Eufemio Zapata in *Viva Zapata!* In 1957, he'd win the Oscar again for his support-ing role as artist Paul Gauguin in Vincente Minnelli's *Lust for Life* (1956). Quinn's third Oscar nomination, and first for Best Actor, came the following year for his role in the box office hit *Wild Is the Wind* (1957). Quinn continued to receive star bill-ing in a number of major motion pictures, culminating in his fourth and final nomination, and second for Best Actor, for his role in *Zorba the Greek* (1964). Though he would resist being pigeonholed, he was continually cast in films featuring ethnic characters. In 1987, he received the Golden Globe's Cecil B. DeMille Award.

In 1962, Rita Moreno—born Rosa Dolores Alverio Marcano in Puerto Rico—became the first Latina to win an Oscar when she received the Best Supporting Actress award for her role as Anita in *West Side Story*. Moreno's long career began at age eleven when she broke into film dubbing Spanish-language versions of American films. By age thirteen she appeared on Broadway in the play *Skydrift*, costarring with Eli Wallach and Arthur Keegan. She became the first Latina actor considered an EGOT for winning Emmy, Grammy, Oscar, and Tony awards—an individual feat that overshadowed the limited opportunities that exist for other Latina/o actors. Like other Latina actresses, Moreno would be stereotyped as hypersexual, as the *Life Magazine* cover she was featured on in 1954 suggested with the line: "Rita Moreno: An Actress's Catalog of Sex and Innocence."[15] A bare-shouldered Moreno, her back to the camera, coquettishly looks into the camera over her shoulder. Moreno's career was shadowed by offers to play exotic or stereotypical roles that she found demeaning. Over the years she has managed to break the mold by depicting a range of characters, including opera star Maria Callas and a southern belle in the play *The Glass Menagerie*. In 2004, her work on film and stage was recognized by President George W. Bush, who presented her the Presidential Medal of Freedom. President Barack Obama later awarded her the National Medal of the Arts, and in 2013 she was given the Screen Actors Guild Life Achievement Award.

The perception that people of color continue to be marginalized and stereotyped in Hollywood has been conclusively documented in a number of studies. *Hollywood Diversity Report 2018: Five Years of Progress and Missed Opportunities*, a study conducted by UCLA, examined the top two hundred theatrical releases in 2016 and 1,251 broadcast, cable, and digital shows from the 2015–2016 season to assess diversity in front of and behind the camera and its impact on the bottom line. The study found minorities disproportionately underrepresented in every category, with 13.9 percent in lead film roles, 12.6 percent as directors, 12.9 percent as digital scripted leads, 8.1 percent as film writers, and about 7 percent as creators of cable or broadcast scripted shows.

Racial minorities were represented at the greatest numbers as leads for broadcast reality shows (26.6 percent), cable reality (20.9 percent), and cable scripted leads (20.2 percent).

And though Black film actors, at 12.5 percent, achieved proportional representation, Latinos—the largest ethnic minority, comprising 18 percent of the US population—were severely underrepresented, with only 2.7 percent of lead roles.

Meanwhile, non-Hispanic Whites, comprising roughly 61 percent of the US population, took 78.1 percent of lead film roles. The share of films with minority–majority casts remained steady over the five years of study; it was 9.9 percent in 2011 and 9.8 percent in 2016.

The findings sparked calls for a boycott of Paramount Pictures, which the National Latino Media Council and the National Hispanic Media Coalition cited as the worst offender. The council's report *Lack of Latinx in the Film Industry* focused on the top-grossing films between 2016 and 2017 and found that Paramount did not release any films featuring a Hispanic writer or lead actor.

"It's a disgrace," said Alex Nogales, the president and CEO of the National Hispanic Media Coalition. "It isn't about actors having a job. This is a civil rights issue. This is about the perception of Latinos. How we are perceived is how we are treated," he said of the group's virtual invisibility despite its large and growing numbers.[16]

Nogales said another persistent problem facing Hispanics in the industry is the importation of talent from abroad. "We have fifty-seven million Latinos in the United States, but we don't exist for them. They go and bring them over here. Four out of five [Oscar winners] have been a Mexican director. When these Mexican directors are getting awards, I'm the first one to cheer, but they're not taking Latino Americans seriously. It's disappointing."[17]

After launching a boycott, Nogales, along with representatives of the National Latino Media Council, met with Paramount COO Andrew Gumpert in October 2018 and presented a petition with twelve thousand names, demanding that studio heads sign a Memorandum of Understanding, a nonbinding agreement, to address the historic exclusion of Latinos in front of and behind the camera. Gumpert declined to sign the agreement. In a statement to the *Hollywood Reporter*, a Paramount spokesperson would only say that he met with the group "in a good faith effort to see how we could partner as we further drive Paramount's culture of diversity, inclusion and belonging."[18] The statement said that Paramount had continued to make progress under a new leadership team and cited a number of upcoming films that demonstrated its commitment to fairer representation.

In February 2019 Paramount announced plans to increase diversity across story lines, vendors and crews. "We have been taken for granted," Nogales said, noting that Latinos comprise 26 percent of ticket buyers but are virtually invisible in film or on the set.[19]

Inclusion or Invisibility?, a 2016 study of diversity in entertainment by the USC Annenberg School for Communication and

Journalism, found that the overwhelming majority of directors were White, representing 87.3 percent of directing jobs in film, 90.4 percent in broadcast, 83.2 percent in cable, and 88.6 percent in streaming. It evaluated 414 stories in top-grossing films across television and film and found that only 12 percent were racially balanced, meaning they nearly reflected the nation's racial composition. In the films assessed, 20.7 percent included underrepresented minorities in speaking roles, which is 16 percent below their composition of the population, based on the US Census.

"Characters from underrepresented racial/ethnic groups are excluded or erased from mediated storytelling," the study said and noted that more than 50 percent of stories featured no speaking Asian characters, and 22 percent featured no speaking Black characters.

"The complete absence of individuals from these backgrounds is a symptom of a diversity strategy that relies on tokenistic inclusion rather than integration," it said. "No platform presents a profile of race/ethnicity that matches proportional representation in the U.S."[20]

The report *Inequality in 900 Popular Films: Examining Portrayals of Gender, Race/Ethnicity, LGBT, and Disability from 2007 to 2016*, released by USC's Media, Diversity, and Social Change Initiative at the Annenberg School, examined nine hundred films released from 2007 to 2016. Of the top one hundred films in 2016, forty-seven had no Black female characters, sixty-six had no Asian female characters, and seventy-two had no Hispanic female characters.[21] In contrast, eleven of the top one hundred movies excluded White females.[22]

Compounding the "inclusion crisis" was the low percentage of speaking characters of color, particularly Hispanics. The percentage of Black speaking characters was 13.6 percent, compared to 5.7 percent Asian—both of which reflected their proportion of the population. But only 3 percent of Latino characters had speaking roles, while 97 percent were silent.

Across the nine hundred films, 3 percent of the directors were Asian or Asian American, and 5.6 percent—a total of fifty-six directors—were Black.

The study said that there had been no significant change in the percentage of non-White characters since 2007. "Hollywood is still so White," it concluded.

"Inclusion in the Director's Chair: Gender, Race, & Age of Directors Across 1,200 Top Films from 2007 to 2018," another USC report, released in 2019, found that only 4 percent of directors were women, while 6 percent were Black, and 3.1 percent Asian. And while Black directors had made significant gains in 2018, their numbers across the twelve years remained disproportionately low, with Black women barely represented at all. During that period, 80 of 1,335 directors were Black.

> Overall, intersectionality is a large problem in the director's chair. Women of color received very few opportunities across the 12-year time frame. Only 9 directing assignments have been filled by women of color across 1,200 top-grossing pictures. These jobs were held by seven women, 4 of which were Black, two Asian, and 1 Latina. Only 2 women of color [Ava DuVernay and Jennifer Yuh Nelson] have helmed 2 motion pictures in the sample time frame.[23]

Earlier USC studies showed that Black directors most often worked on films featuring Black casts, which often limited their opportunities, but the crossover success of films like *Black*

Panther, *Girls Trip*, and *Hidden Figures* could indicate either change or a statistical blip caused by a handful of hits. Either way, USC's 2019 "Inclusion" study showed that the four Black female directors of the one hundred top-grossing films in 2018 represented less than 1 percent of all directors.

"It's dismal," said Gina Prince-Bythewood, one of the handful of female writers and directors of color working in the industry. She attributes much of the problem to the lack of diversity among studio executives able to green-light projects. The 2015 *Hollywood Diversity Report* found that 96 percent of TV studio chairs and/or CEOs, and 92 percent of senior management, is White. Prince-Bythewood, who is African American, said she is typically the only person of color in the room when pitching a project. "It's wrong and not smart," she said. "You're seeing and hearing pitches from one perspective."[24]

Prince-Bythewood recalled her protracted struggle to get studio backing for her first film, *Love and Basketball*, a partly autobiographical story about her time as a young basketball player who "falls in love with the boy next door." "Every single production company and every single studio passed," said Prince-Bythewood, a graduate of the USC Film School who had left a job as a television writer to devote time to her script. The final rejection was by the company owned by the actress Jodie Foster. "I was completely devastated. I spent a year and a half writing it. Now what was I going to do?"[25]

But within days of that rebuff she received a call from someone at the Sundance Writers Lab who had heard about the script. Prince-Bythewood applied and secured a spot in the program.

"I had incredible mentors who gave me thoughts on the script. I rewrote it and Sundance put on a reading of it."

Among the industry people invited to the reading was someone from 40 Acres, director Spike Lee's production company, which took the script to New Line Cinema. Prince-Bythewood recalls sitting outside the office of Michael De Luca, the New Line president. To settle her nerves, she walked into his office as she would a basketball court.

"The first thing he said is, 'This was one of the best love stories I ever read.' There were no questions about me directing. He asked how much money I needed. I said $10 million, he said, 'No, you need more.' It was an incredible moment."

It was a moment made possible due to the intervention of Lee's company. "It was a production company—a Black production company—that could identify with the value of the story and could leverage its power and relationships to get it made."

The film, now considered a classic, premiered at the 2000 Sundance Film Festival and in 2001 won the prestigious Independent Spirit Award for Best First Screenplay. It was also nominated for Best First Feature and won the 2000 Humanitas Prize, which recognizes film and television writing that recognizes human dignity and freedom. The film also grossed $27.4 million and had the second highest-grossing opening weekend.

"My fight is to get the industry to look at films with people of color as the specific genre—they're comedies, period pieces, biopics—as opposed to a 'Black film,'" Prince-Bythewood said.

"Are they good characters? That's what should matter."[26]

While there are exceptions—among them Shonda Rhimes, who has become one of television's most successful creators—history suggests that that kind of assessment would require changes in the studio executive suites. "It's going to take a change in leadership and diversifying the ranks of people who can green-light projects," she said.

"It comes down to understanding the culture," offered director George Tillman Jr., whose string of films include *The Hate U Give* (2018), *Barbershop* and its sequels (2002, 2004, 2016), *Men of Honor* (2000), and *Soul Food* (1997), the latter his debut film that he wrote and directed. Tillman recalls how studio executives had a difficult time relating to his pitch of *Barbershop*, a story that centers on a shop on the south side of Chicago that is the lifeblood of the neighborhood. "They didn't see how this could be successful," he said of the film starring Ice Cube, produced by Tillman, and directed by Tim Story. The film went on to inspire two sequels and a television show, and though it cost $12 million to make, it grossed more than $77 million globally. "You have to explain," Tillman said. "It's always a battle."[27]

Tillman's 2018 film *The Hate U Give*, which he directed, tells the story of a young Black girl navigating her poor, urban neighborhood and her rich, mostly White private school world who witnesses the police shooting of her best friend. "It's a personal film for me," Tillman said. "It's one of the few things I did for myself. It was significantly important to the culture. It's what I wanted to do, regardless of the outcome."[28]

He knew it would be difficult to get a major studio to back a film that addresses racially charged issues, among them police violence against Blacks, the infiltration of drugs in under-resourced communities, the values of the Black Panther Party, and code-switching—the way Blacks negotiate Black and

White worlds. His case was strengthened by the popularity of the best-selling book of the same title and the recent critical and commercial success of films such as *Get Out* and *Moonlight*, both featuring Black characters and themes and directed by Black filmmakers.

Director Malcolm Lee, whose string of films have included *Girls Trip* (2017), *The Best Man Holiday* (2013), and *The Best Man* (1999), has repeatedly proven the viability of films with predominantly Black casts.

The Best Man, his debut film with characters that mirrored his own middle-class background, exceeded box office tracking projections by opening at Number 1. Fourteen years later, the $17 million sequel *The Best Man Holiday* again stunned the industry by opening at Number 2 and having the fifth-largest opening for an R-rated romantic comedy ever. It was also the second-highest opening for an urban romantic comedy and received an A+ CinemaScore. Opening weekend receipts nearly doubled the film's $17 million budget, and it was barely edged out by *Thor*, which cost $150 million to make.

The 2018 *Hollywood Diversity Report* found that the industry routinely undersells the relatively small number of films with diverse leads and casts "in a global market that is primed to connect with them."[29] Instead, it said the majority of films and television shows continue to have casts that are 10 percent minority or less, "despite the fact that these projects are collectively among the poorest performs."[30]

It said that films with 21 to 30 percent minority casts enjoyed the highest median global box office receipts, and global return on investment peaked for films with casts that were

41–50 percent minority, while films with the most racial homo-geneity were the poorest performers.

"The previous reports in this series dispel a stubborn Holly-wood myth that in order to reach the widest audiences possible, films and television shows must center White characters in their narratives and relegate racial and ethnic others to, at best, sup-porting roles," the report said."[31]

But in Hollywood, racial mythology trumps reality, and the president of distribution at Universal expressed surprise over *The Best Man Holiday*'s strong opening, which she had underesti-mated by half. As a *Time* magazine article said, "The response to the surprise smash was breathless."[32]

Such low expectations continually plague films by filmmakers of color and make every success appear like a fluke, fueling a cycle in which their films are undervalued by studio executives.

"You have to go back to the beginning; you don't get the div-idend from previous films," said Misan Sagay, a Black British filmmaker and member of the Academy of Motion Pictures.[33]

Linda Holmes, entertainment writer for NPR, recoiled at the perception that a film must appeal to a predominantly White audience to be considered a success.

"How broad does an audience have to be before it's just 'an audience'?" Holmes asked, noting that Lee's film opened bigger, at fewer theaters, and without so-called A-list actors, than did *Captain Phillips*, starring Tom Hanks, a film nearly four times as expensive to make.[34]

Lee's 2017 film *Girls Trip*, about four friends taking a week-end trip to the Essence Music Festival, similarly defied expecta-tion by becoming the first film written, directed, produced, and starring Blacks to cross the $100 million domestic box office total, which it did in its fourth week. (The writer was Tracy Oliver.) It was also the year's highest-grossing R-rated comedy and raised Lee's profile in the status-obsessed industry.

"I think there's a low bar of expectation because the movies don't cost a lot to make," Lee said. "So there's not as much pressure on a movie. They leave you alone."[35] But, he added, "they often underestimate the audience desire to see themselves onscreen."

Lee's characters are typically educated, attractive, and successful, and eschew the crude one-dimensional Black characters long a staple in Hollywood. A study by the University of Southern California's Viterbi School of Engineering used artificial intelligence to analyze nearly one thousand popular recent film scripts. It found that many films that feature minorities continue to reinforce stereotypes, with African American characters more likely to curse and Latino characters more likely to discuss sexuality.

Growing up in a middle-class family in Brooklyn's Crown Heights section, Lee was always struck by the limited roles for African Americans in film. "John Singleton and the Hughes brothers were making movies about violence in the 'hood. I didn't grow up that way," he said, a reference to movies like *Boyz N the Hood* (1991), *Menace II Society* (1993), and *Dead Presidents* (1995), which explored the gritty side of Black urban life.

"Whether it was a Hughes Brothers movie or the Black guy who was the sidekick, or the educated Black person who was a sellout," Lee said he did not see images of middle-class African Americans like him who attended private schools but who also took immense pride in their African American heritage.[36] Still, those films stoked his ambitions.

"I remember seeing *Boyz N the Hood* and being very inspired by it," he said of the film for which John Singleton, at age twenty-three, became the youngest and the first African American nominated for an Oscar for Best Director. "I didn't relate to hearing gunfire while I was doing my homework but could relate to a story that was personal and could be told on a large platform."

"I wanted to see myself represented on screen and make universal films that have Black faces in them," Lee said. "Films that have cultural specificity but were universal—everyone has a coming of age story. Everyone has weddings, gatherings."

Lee attended New York University Tisch School of the Arts, where he made his first film, *Morningside Prep*, which was loosely based on his experience attending an exclusive private school. *The Best Man* (1999), which he wrote and directed, is about a group of college friends who reunite for a friend's wedding. It was produced by his cousin, filmmaker Spike Lee.

"I try to ground it in reality and find what's authentic about African American culture from my perspective. I hadn't seen that growing up."

Despite the economic and critical success of films by Lee and other filmmakers of color, their projects are a harder sell and often fail to command the big budgets that films by their White counterparts do.

"They've got people on the inside who are advocating for those movies," Lee said. "They have people that are fighting for them—the studio execs, the influential agents, the stars themselves—rarely are they Black."

The dearth of films by people of color has resulted in fewer that become contenders for Oscars and other top prizes.

Filmmakers of color are hoping that films such as *Moonlight* (2016) and *Black Panther* (2018) will convince studios of their artistic and commercial potential. *Moonlight* won Best Picture, and Barry Jenkins was nominated for Best Director and, with Terrell Alvin McCraney, won for Best Adapted Screenplay. The film was also nominated for Best Supporting Actor, Best Supporting Actress, and Cinematography.

Tillman's *The Hate U Give* received nearly universal accolades. *Variety* called it "the rare racial drama that will detonate the complacency of even those who are drawn to see it. It's that good, that searching, that fierce in its humanity," and *Fortune* hailed it as an "Oscar-worthy Masterpiece."[37]

Still, it was overlooked by the Academy. But Tillman had not been holding his breath, given the decades of award-worthy films by Black directors that had been overlooked. "You think back—*Malcolm X* (1992) didn't get nominated. *Do the Right Thing*," he said, referring to two films directed by Spike Lee.[38] While *Do the Right Thing* (1989) was nominated for Best Screenplay, the snub for Best Director or Best Picture triggered controversy and a rebuke by Academy Awards host Kim Basinger, who remarked on the omission while presenting the award for Best Picture. Some found the oversight particularly jarring given its juxtaposition that year with *Driving Miss Daisy* (1989), a film about an elderly White woman and her Black chauffeur that played into centuries-old stereotypes of Black servitude. It won the award for Best Picture. "All these great films. That tells you who is controlling things all these years," Tillman said.[39]

In 1997, Tim Reid, with his wife actress Daphne Reid, founded New Millennium Studios, a film production studio in Virginia that they operated for nearly twenty years.

"William Paley said something I'll never forget and is why I built a studio," Reid said of the founder of CBS. "He said, 'What is your propaganda?' This is a man who created TV network news, who gave Walter Cronkite his job, and he's asking me what's my propaganda. That's when I decided to build a studio to build my own cultural propaganda. I was in his office for twenty minutes—if he's telling me there's power in the images, then I'd better listen and understand. I'm a cultural propagandist. Culture has been in the hands of a very small group of people and that's not helpful for the culture of Black America. How do we get our cultural strength to benefit our children, our community? How do we fight the constant bombardment of negative images?"[40]

Reid said the film *Hidden Figures* (2016), which told the story of the African American women who worked at NASA, brought tears to his eyes "out of pride and anger. I had to be seventy to find this out. Imagine if that story had been taught in grade school, what kind of dreams they could have inspired. They would know the incredible things these people did against all odds . . . These are incredible stories that young Black people should know so they can dream bigger dreams. When you control the message you control the mind of people. It's the most powerful force on this planet."

In 2016, Spike Lee and actors Will Smith and Jada Pinkett Smith boycotted the Oscars to protest the second year in a row in which all the acting nominees were White. Exacerbating the slight was that the only nomination for the film *Straight Outta Compton* (2015), a film directed by African director F. Gary Gray about the rap group N.W.A., was for the White screenwriter. Ryan Coogler, the Black writer and director of *Creed*, was also overlooked, though the film's White star, Sylvester Stallone, was nominated. Coogler would go on to direct the 2018 blockbuster *Black Panther*.

"Mean no disrespect to my friends, host Chris Rock and Producer Reggie Hudlin, President Isaacs and the Academy," Lee wrote in an Instagram post, "but how is it possible for the second consecutive year all 20 contenders under the actor category are White? And let's not even get into the other branches. 40 White actors in two years and no flava at all. We can't act? WTF!"[41]

Cheryl Boone Isaacs, who in 2013 became the first African American president of the Academy of Motion Picture Arts and Sciences, issued a statement saying that while she acknowledged the wonderful work of that year's nominees, "I am both heartbroken and frustrated about the lack of inclusion. This is a difficult but important conversation, and it's time for big changes."[42]

Months earlier, the Academy had adopted "A2020," a five-year diversity initiative to increase the number of women, minorities, and international members in the Academy by 2020. But as controversy swirled, the Academy board members held an emergency session in January 2016 and voted unanimously to diversify the voting body by recruiting new members while moving those who had been inactive in film the previous ten years to "emeritus" status. A similar strategy had been used in 1970 by then-president of the Academy Gregory Peck to bring in younger voting members to make the organization more current. The latest purge triggered a backlash. David Kirkpatrick, producer of film classics *Reds* and *Terms of Endearment*, accused the Academy of "exchanging purported racism with ageism."[43]

Boone Isaacs conceded the strategy was imperfect and would not alone fix the problem but said, "The change is not coming as fast as we would like. We need to do more, and better and more quickly."[44]

"The Academy has a problem," actor David Oyelowo said during remarks at the King Legacy Awards where Boone Isaacs received the Rosa Parks Humanitarian Award. A year earlier, Oyelowo's critically acclaimed role as Rev. Martin Luther King Jr. in *Selma* (2014), directed by DuVernay, was among those that the Academy had overlooked.[45] In 2017, upon ending her four-year term as president, Boone Isaacs announced that she would not seek reelection to the Academy board on which she had served for nearly a quarter century. By 2019, the Academy had reached its goal of 16 percent by doubling the proportion of voting members of color, a number that Reign called "completely arbitrary. Why that number?"[46]

Even so, during the 2019 Oscar season, the nominees appeared more diverse than ever and included Spike Lee for his film *Black KKKlansman* (2018), based on the true story of a Black detective who infiltrated the Ku Klux Klan; *Green Book* (2018), named for the guidebook used by Blacks to travel through segregated parts of the country; *Black Panther* (2018); *If Beale Street Could Talk*, based on a James Baldwin novel; and *Roma* (2018), which tells the story of an indigenous live-in maid working in an affluent household in Mexico City. The night still ended in controversy when *Green Book* won for Best Picture. The film was based on the story of Dr. Don Shirley, an African American musical prodigy, and his travels through the Deep South in the 1960s. However, Shirley's story was overshadowed by the film's focus on his alleged interracial friendship with his White driver, who Shirley's family say was exaggerated. Noting how the film played into a familiar Hollywood trope of the Great White Savior, some called it the era's *Driving Miss Daisy*. Critics also complained that while the film was named for the seminal guidebook that African American motorists found essential during a period when many hotels and restaurants would not serve them, it is hardly mentioned in the film.

As the White male director and producers rushed to the stage to accept the awards for *Green Book*, Lee, whose film had also been nominated and who had earlier won for Best Adapted Screenplay, stormed from his seat and tried to exit the auditorium.[47]

Reid said those who are in positions of power must not be afraid to rock the boat. Tillman agreed. "We need to use our voice, our votes, we're in the unions, we can run. That's the only way."

In the meantime, directors such as Tillman and Malcolm Lee regularly employ a stable of actors who are rarely cast in big-budget films. Lee said the actors in *The Best Man* and its sequel are among the most talented and undervalued performers in Hollywood. He said that he's unable to offer them the contracts they deserve. The cast, who became known as "the Black Pack," included Taye Diggs, Regina Hall, Morris Chestnut, Sanaa Lathan, Terrence Howard, and Nia Long. In 2018, Hall became the first African American actor in the eight-decade history of the New York Film Critics Circle to win its coveted Best Actress award.

E. Brian Dobbins, the executive producer of *Black-ish* and one of the few managers of color in Hollywood, believes the low starting pay and nonexistent farm system for people of color deters many from the business. The industry is known for its insularity and nepotism, with generations of the same families working in front of and behind the camera. He said many college-educated minorities feel compelled to take a safer route to success.

"I was the first in my immediate family to graduate college. They thought I should be an attorney," said Dobbins, the grandson of a former sharecropper.[48] "I made a sharp left turn from what their expectation was. They didn't say don't do that—but I still felt the pressure being a Black young man who had gone to college, I had to make something of myself. You have to go make money and help take care of your family. I come out of college and go into entertainment and see no one who looks like me who's made it—no one is running a studio, is head of an agency, successful producers, managers. There wasn't a Jackie Robinson for me to be inspired by. I was very much discouraged. It's a hard business. You start in the mailroom and make no money. If you see the light at the end of the tunnel, you keep putting those thorns in your hands. I just kept going in spite of it. I'm not a quitter. I just felt I'm going to figure it out."

Dobbins went on to describe a familiar scenario in creative fields where low-paying apprenticeships become a barrier to entry for those lacking wealth and connections. "I felt like an outsider looking in," he said of his first nine months working in the mailroom at United Talent Agency. "People I started with had made their way to the desk. I was as capable, as poised. What I didn't have was anyone I could go to for advice. As the only Black male I felt there was more of a spotlight on me. I worked hard. I knew I could do the job. I just didn't know how to [seek out advice] without feeling like I was losing my dignity."

Dobbins eventually worked his way out of the mailroom where he came to realize the unique role he could play in the careers of actors and directors of color. "What I noticed was that people of color were represented but not appreciated in the way I thought they should be appreciated. Somebody that I appreciate from my community that is an artist performing in a way that I appreciate may not be the same for everyone . . . It's just that if you are a person of color you deserve somebody who is going to be out there fighting for you—you should have access to someone who appreciates who you are and where you come from. I started seeing people that UTA represented and there was never any reverence for people that were important to me."

While the artists of color were being represented and protected, he did not believe the breadth of their talent or their value in the marketplace was fully recognized. "Our business working with artists in film and TV, so much is subjective," he said.

"A lot of time you're educating people about what is being bought and developed. The role is to fight for your artist . . . and create a path."

Dobbins's roster of clients has included Regina Hall; director F. Gary Gray, *Straight Outta Compton* (2015) and *The Fate of the Furious* (2017); and Kenya Barris, the creator and writer of *Black-ish*, along with cast members Tracee Ellis Ross and Anthony Anderson.

Dobbins said there are opportunities in the field for people of color but many are unfamiliar with the business side of the industry. "You need role models. A lot of people just don't even know what I do."

Sagay agrees and believes her generation of filmmakers should have done more to develop the pipeline. "We in the vanguard sort of failed for people coming up behind us. It should be easier for them. I'm not sure we've done that. Several people I'm mentoring say they're repeating what I experienced. That doesn't feel right at all. There should have been a cohort of people coming up. That just doesn't seem to be the case. One remains the unicorn."[49] On the other hand, the handful of directors of color who break through must take on the added burden of promoting diversity when many themselves still face a host of challenges in an industry in which they remain undervalued.

Another impediment for filmmakers and actors of color is the lack of diversity among film critics. *Critic's Choice: Gender and Race/Ethnicity of Film Reviewers*, a 2018 study by USC, examined 19,559 reviews of the top one hundred films of 2017. It found that White critics authored 82 percent of reviews and noted that the dearth of reviewers of color can have a deleterious effect on audience behavior and ticket sales. White male critics wrote substantially more reviews—63.9 percent, compared to 18 percent for White female, 13.8 percent underrepresented male, and only 4.1 percent underrepresented female. On average, 14.2 reviews were written by White male critics, compared to 11.1 by underrepresented male critics; 9.4 by White female critics; and 5.6 by underrepresented female critics.

Seventy percent or more male critics reviewed 69 percent of films with female leads.

In films with underrepresented lead actors, none featured a proportionate share of diverse critics. Top critics—or those deemed so by Rotten Tomatoes—wrote a total of 3,359 reviews across the one hundred movies, with 76 percent written by males and 24 percent by females. White critics' reviews (88.8 percent) outnumbered those from underrepresented racial/ethnic groups (11.2 percent) nearly eight to one.

"While male critics were writing top film reviews at a rate of nearly 27 times their underrepresented female counterparts," the study said. "The consequences of this skewed representation must be considered—what are the ramifications of having cultural storytelling produced and evaluated largely by individuals from the same demographic group. How does this perpetuate a worldview that may not be shared by the more diverse ticket-buying audience at the box office?"[50]

"The dearth of underrepresented women is startling in its own right, but more so when considering the invisibility of women and girls of color on screen in film." The exclusion of critics of color, then, perpetuates the misrepresentation and marginalization of women of color in film by muting the voices that would be most inclined to call it out.

Brie Larson, the Oscar winner and star of *Captain Marvel* (2019), in response to negative reviews of *A Wrinkle in Time* (2018), said: "I don't need a White dude to tell me what didn't work for him about *A Wrinkle in Time*."[51] The film, starring Oprah Winfrey and directed by Ava DuVernay, was the first film with a budget beyond nine figures directed by a woman of color. "It wasn't made for him. I want to know what that film meant to women of color, to biracial women, to teen women of color, to teens that are biracial."[52]

Some reviewers came under fire for their characterization of Holiday. *USA Today* described *The Best Man Holiday* as "race-themed," and *Entertainment Weekly* called *The Best Man* "The Big Chill for the African American Audience," thus marginalizing its appeal beyond Black viewers. The "Critic's Choice" study suggested that film aggregator sites like Rotten Tomatoes and Metacritic address disparities in critic representation by ensuring parity in the critics they include in their rating summaries. "Engaging in further efforts to court those writers to post to the site and including their thoughts in the average rating . . . is imperative."[53] The sites could also identify the race/ethnicity or LGBTQ and disability status of the reviewers—particularly in reviews for films with underrepresented lead characters.

Stacy L. Smith, a professor of film and the founding director of the Inclusion Initiative at USC's Annenberg School for Communication and Journalism, said the industry needed to rely on "evidence-based solutions" to address the trend of underrepresentation. She called on studio executives, producers, and agents to adopt the Rooney Rule, an NFL policy that stipulates that people from underrepresented groups be included as candidates for coaching jobs. The rule resulted in an increase in the number of minority coaches in the NFL (see chapter 7). "By cooperating to expand the talent considered for top film jobs, agents, managers, executives, and producers can work from the top down to create change," stated the report "Inclusion in the Director's Chair," which Smith coauthored in 2017.[54] She called on A-list actors to support inclusion by adding equity riders to their contracts. Among those who support the practice are director J. J. Abrams and actors/producers Ben Affleck, Matt Damon, Paul Feil, and Michael B. Jordan.

But Sagay said the issue of diversity goes beyond numbers. "There's still a perception you're hiring a color and not a writer. If the script has White leads they don't hire you. If it's a lead with a Black woman, they'll still hire a White writer."[55] As a result, she said, the progression common for White filmmakers who begin in writers' rooms and progress through the system doesn't exist for many people of color.

"Other filmmakers are being nurtured in the system," Sagay said. "A lot of young filmmakers had the training and then they're still not hired. A lot of the young Black writers have to work outside the system. That is a much harder path because while you are really honing your craft you're not being paid. I was lucky but it shouldn't be about being lucky. There's a career progression. If you don't get writing jobs, if you don't have people you know already, if you don't have wealthy parents, it's hard."

"People want diversity as long as they don't have to do it," Sagay added. "A lot of the times they want our physical presence but not our voice. So that's the problem. You need a real structural change. I need to be able to walk in and there should be some brown faces when I'm pitching. Until there's diversity at every level, I doubt filmmakers of color will be on a level playing field."

Tillman said it was Damon Wayans's insistence on diversity on the film crew for his film *Mo' Money* (1992) that's responsible for his break into the film industry. Fresh out of college, Tillman was hired as a dresser, the person who arranges items on the set. "At that time, there weren't enough African Americans working in the union. Who's the lighter? Who's the grip? A lot of people use people they have relationships with. It's the people they're used to working with. You have to break that. When I see him I say, 'Thank you. You don't understand how much that changed my life.'"[56]

CHAPTER

3

RAGING TOWERS

*"It is a hard thing to live haunted by the ghost of
an untrue dream."*
—W. E. B. Du Bois, *The Souls of Black Folk,* 1903

By the time news of student protests at Yale commanded
national headlines in November 2015, the "White girls
only" fraternity party was only the latest in a series of alleged
offences against students of color. For years, students had complained to administrators about a campus climate in which
they felt unwelcome, unsafe, and alienated, both in and out of
the classroom. In 2014, students had found swastikas outside a
freshman dorm, and in November 2015, just days after female
students of color claimed they were turned away from a "White
girls only" fraternity party, they received threats and felt compelled to reschedule a forum on race. Two days later, during the
rescheduled forum, students shared wrenching stories about

racial insensitivity and the paucity of Black faculty. The next day, roughly three hundred students gathered around Jonathan Holloway, a professor of African American history who in 2014 had become the college's first African American dean.

"As a Black man, you know where we come from," one African American student said. "You need to act. We need you."[1]

Holloway was mostly silent as he listened and at times took notes. "It's not easy to hear your stories," he finally said. "It's difficult to know that someone who's vested with the responsibility to take care of everybody, that you felt the need to tell me that. It's painful for me, but I'm glad you did."[2]

Holloway said he had tried to address some of the issues they raised behind the scenes but conceded his efforts had not been enough. "I'll do better. I want you to know that I'm going to try my damnedest."

Similar protests played out at college campuses across the country, where students of color complained that their daily experiences and history went unacknowledged in conversations and campus events and in the curriculum in environments where faculty and administrators of color are rare and White professors appear ill equipped or reluctant to engage matters of race.

At Yale, the culminating event was a mass email to students sent out by Erika Christakis, an associate master of one of Yale's fourteen residential colleges. In response to an email from school officials urging students to avoid racially offensive Halloween costumes, including head feathers and blackface, she wrote:

> I wonder, and I am not trying to be provocative. Is there no room anymore for a child or young person to be a little bit obnoxious . . . a little bit inappropriate or provocative or, yes,

offensive? . . . Have we lost faith in young people's capacity—
in your capacity—to exercise self-censure through social norm-
ing and also in your capacity to ignore or reject things that
trouble you?[3]

She added that her husband, Nicholas, a physician, sociologist,
and master of Yale's Silliman College—which happened to be
named for a former professor from a prosperous slaveholding
family—said, "If you don't like a costume someone is wearing,
look away, or tell them you are offended. Talk to each other. Free
speech and the ability to tolerate offence are the hallmarks of a
free and open society."[4]

The email provoked days of protests and demands by some
for the removal of Christakis, a lecturer at the Yale Child Study
Center. National columnists, including George Will at the
Washington Post, entered the fray, defending her First Amendment right to free speech and characterizing the Black students
as overly sensitive. Yale president Peter Salovey sparked criticism
in some conservative circles after word got out that, in a private
meeting with African American students, he took responsibility
for the outcry.

"We failed you," he reportedly told some forty students. "I
think we have to be a better university. I think we have to do
a better job."[5] Salovey, in the end, stood by Christakis and her
husband, saying they would remain at the college, even though
she ultimately decided to step down from her teaching role and
her husband announced he was going on sabbatical. Both eventually resigned from their college residency roles.

On November 6—a week after the controversial email sparked
outrage—Holloway finally responded to the escalating unrest in

a written statement in which he said he had been moved to tears a day earlier by the student testimonials. "I write too late for too many of you, I freely admit," wrote Holloway. "I heard every word that was spoken and I watched every tear that was shed." Holloway vowed to "uphold your right to speak and be heard . . . I will enforce the community standards that safeguard you as members of this community. I do this as I hold us all, including myself, accountable to give what we seek: respect."[6]

That same year, at Harvard Law School, portraits of African American professors in Wasserstein Hall were defaced with black tape. Black student activists believed the incident was in retaliation for their campaign to change the school crest, which is modeled on the coat of arms of Isaac Royall Jr., a slaveholder who helped found and finance the school. The student group demanded the "decolonization" of the campus, including its curriculum. At a community meeting, Harvard Law School dean Martha Minow decried the event as abhorrent and acknowledged that racism was a "serious problem" in the school as it is nationally. Minow issued a statement saying: "We are focused on efforts to improve our community, examining structures that may contribute to negative experiences of any members of our community, and pursuing opportunities where the School can both change and support change."[7]

Also in 2015, at the University of Missouri, the president and chancellor resigned amid protests, including a student hunger strike, a boycott of classes by students and faculty, and a threatened football team boycott over the administration's failure to respond to a number of racial incidents on campus. Among them was the placement of cotton balls in front of the Black Culture Center and episodes in which racial slurs were hurled

at a Black student who was president of MU's student government by Whites in a pickup truck and, in a separate incident, at
the Legion of Black Collegians as they prepared for homecom-
ing activities. Students were also troubled by the administration's silence in the wake of the 2014 police shooting of Michael
Brown, an African American teenager, in nearby Ferguson, Missouri. In the midst of protests, human feces was used to draw a
swastika on a wall.

Upon resigning, University of Missouri president Tim Wolfe
conceded he should have spoken out sooner. "The frustration,
the anger I see is clear, it's real. We didn't respond or react. We
got frustrated with each other, and we forced individuals like
Jonathan Butler," the student on the hunger strike, "to take
immediate action and unusual steps to effect change."[8] Following the resignations, Michael Middleton, an African American
alumnus and former deputy chancellor, was appointed to serve
as interim president, and the university for the first time hired a
chief diversity, inclusion, and equity officer.

Complaints about cultural insensitivity and racism reverber-
ated on campuses across the country, including New York University, where students at the Greenwich Village campus gave
tearful testimonials about their experiences during an hours-
long town hall meeting attended by the university president,
the provost, and other top administrators. The following year,
the university's new president, Andrew Hamilton, appointed a
diversity task force and in 2017 appointed a senior vice president
for Global Inclusion, Diversity, and Strategic Innovation, the
university's inaugural chief diversity officer.

Meanwhile, an epidemic of parties and other campus events
featuring White students in blackface or otherwise mocking

African Americans—such as the "Bullets and Bubbly" party at the University of Connecticut Law School—were reported around the country. At Syracuse University, the student newspaper uncovered a fraternity initiation rite that required inductees to utter racial slurs. These were not isolated incidents. The US Department of Education said there had been a 25 percent increase in reported hate crimes on campus between 2015 and 2016.

Two-Faced Racism, an analysis of several hundred students' journals by Leslie Houts Picca, found that such events were commonplace.[9] The revelation in 2019 that Virginia governor Ralph Northam and the state attorney general may have also donned blackface in college indicated how deeply entrenched the practice is and the extent to which White students today are following a long tradition.[10]

The more recent protests highlighted the unfinished business of diversity efforts that had begun in the 1960s when Black students demanded more faculty of color and curricula that moved beyond a Eurocentric canon. While the earlier protests had resulted in the creation of programs like Black studies, most schools have done little to address the core curricula or expose how America's carefully constructed racial caste system has created and maintained inequality. This historical void has left many White Americans unable to see how a deeply embedded ideology of White superiority and Black inferiority continues to warp racial perceptions—and perpetuate injustice—today.

The 2015 protests played out as a series of police killings of unarmed African Americans riveted the nation and sparked national conversations about race and inequality in the criminal justice system. Many of these fatal episodes were captured on videotape and broadcast on television news, spawning the movement "Black Lives Matter," which highlighted the systemic failure of the criminal justice system to prosecute or convict officers in even some of the more blatant encounters.

The Black students' sense of alienation on majority-White campuses was buttressed by polls that highlighted the Black–White divide over perceptions of racial injustice. Eighty-six percent of Blacks and just 30 percent of Whites disagreed with the verdict in the killing of Trayvon Martin by a volunteer community patrolman who stalked and fatally shot the unarmed teenager visiting family in Florida. Eighty percent of Blacks and just 23 percent of Whites condemned the decision not to prosecute the officer in the killing of eighteen-year-old Michael Brown in Ferguson, Missouri.[11] And while Eric Garner's illegal chokehold police killing in Staten Island, New York, was caught on camera, 90 percent of Blacks but just 47 percent of Whites polled by the Pew Research Center opposed the grand jury decision not to prosecute.[12]

This steadfast support for police even in the face of obvious instances of misconduct explains the absence of widespread White outrage over unjust policies that resulted in the quadrupling of African American male imprisonment between 1980 and 1999. When surveyed in 2013, just over two-thirds of Blacks but just a little over one-quarter of Whites believed the criminal justice system was biased against Blacks.[13] A more recent Pew survey in 2019 found that 87 percent of Black adults, compared to 61 percent of Whites, believed Blacks are generally treated less fairly by the criminal justice system. And while 79 percent of Blacks surveyed believed the treatment of racial and ethnic minorities by the criminal justice system is a big problem, only 32 percent of Whites shared that view.[14]

In *White Rage,* historian Carol Anderson recounts how during the Reagan administration, as the crack epidemic ravaged Black communities, President Reagan criminalized their inhabitants rather than the drug smugglers and cartels. He signed into law the Anti-Drug Abuse Act that mandated minimum sentencing and that favored punishment over treatment. It also set a one hundred to one disparity in sentencing between crack and cocaine, which disproportionately criminalized African Americans, Latinos, and the poor.

In 1988, Congress enacted mandatory sentencing for even first-time offenders while the Supreme Court, in a series of previous cases, upheld mandatory sentencing for drug offenses, permitted racial profiling by police, and made it more difficult to prove racial bias in a variety of circumstances, including jury selection and arrests.

In 1994, President Bill Clinton signed into law a crime bill long advocated by Republicans that ushered in even harsher mandatory minimum sentencing for low-level offenses and, in many cases, the end of parole, which caused the incarceration of Black males to spike further.

As a result, Blacks, who are 12 percent of the national adult population, are 33 percent of those incarcerated. An ACLU report in 2013 found that Blacks in Baltimore County were up to 5.6 times more likely than Whites to be arrested for marijuana, even though the groups use the drug at the same rate.[15]

Black students confronted with the continuing reality of racial bigotry were on campuses where neither the history nor contemporary challenges of discrimination were engaged in the classroom or by administrators. While many Whites stood silent in the face of stark injustice, they were quick to condemn movements like "Blacks Lives Matter" or NFL player Colin Kaepernick taking a knee in protest. As the movement spilled onto campuses, many Whites were unable to grasp its urgency or nuanced meaning. Many obliviously retorted that *all* lives matter, conveniently neglecting to discern that Black—and not *all*—lives are routinely defiled with impunity. In America, where the sanctity of White life is apparent, it is pointless to insist it matters. At many majority-White campuses, the unspoken message is that for diversity to succeed, students of color must adapt to White indifference to systemic injustice.

"I saw it coming," Michael Middleton said of the 2015 protests at the University of Missouri that resulted in the resignations of the chancellor and president, and resulted in Middleton's appointment as interim president. "These students were making these complaints for a number of years before 2015. The leadership was not responding. The leadership didn't even understand. They thought they were troublemakers. They didn't listen. They didn't have the resources."[16]

As interim president, Middleton's experience at U Missouri had come full circle. In 1968, he was a senior and among the student activists whose demands to school administrators were strikingly similar to those of students of color nearly fifty years later. A native of Mississippi, he was already intimately accustomed to racial segregation before he set foot on the campus. Still, he was taken aback by its similarity to Mississippi. "The difference in Missouri is segregation wasn't by law, but by custom."

He recalled how, on his first day on campus, a passerby shouted, "Go home, n—," out of a car window. "This was a state university, and I was home," he said.

For four years, Middleton had endured the slights experienced by other African American students on campus at that time. He recalled the social isolation at a school where he was often the only African American in classes where his White professors rarely called on him. But Middleton quickly learned his place in the rigidly segregated environment. In the school cafeteria, a small number of African American students were relegated to a corner booth. "The place could be totally crowded but our booth would be empty. We could always find a seat in our booth."

In his senior year, he was among the students who formed the Legion of Black Collegians to draw attention to the paucity of students and faculty of color and the need for Black studies. The group submitted its list of demands to the school—including the hiring of more African American faculty, the establishment of a Black studies program, more scholarships for the recruitment of Black students, and a Black culture center. The school responded by giving the group a dilapidated building on campus to use for gatherings. "We didn't get a Black culture center until the 2000s."

The experience, Middleton said, made him more determined to succeed. He went on to become one of the first three African American graduates of the university law school, where he had found a handful of supportive White professors. In 1985, Middleton became its first African American law professor after working for several years in the Reagan administration with Clarence Thomas in the Equal Employment Opportunity division of the Justice Department. He described an uphill fight against his supervisors over issues of employment discrimination. William

Bradford Reynolds, the US assistant attorney general in charge of the US Department of Justice's Civil Rights Division, did not believe in class action lawsuits to challenge workplace discrimination. "We were fighting about what kind of cases the federal government would bring." He said Thomas, who initially sided with him, ultimately supported the position of the White House.

In 1985, Middleton was hired by Dale A. Whitman, the dean of the University of Missouri School of Law, to teach. Then in 1996, university chancellor Charles Kiesler appointed Middleton to serve as interim vice provost for minority affairs, a position he agreed to take for a year. "I didn't want to permanently be the Black guy doing the Black work," he explained. A short time later he rose to deputy chancellor, a role that included overseeing diversity.

By the time of the 2015 uprising, Middleton was set to retire. "I stayed on to help him with the protest issues that were brewing at the time. They keep dragging me back," he said, noting his appointment as interim president.

As interim president, Middleton was able to hire the university's first chief diversity officer and allocate $7 million for diversity initiatives. Conversely, during the sixteen years that he had served as deputy chancellor, he was unable to muster meaningful university support for diversity initiatives. "As deputy chancellor, I had a number of bosses and people who were at my level in the organization who could say no, put up roadblocks. As president, I [was] the final decision maker," indicating to him the role leadership plays in realizing campus diversity. "It's like having a hair-trigger gun. As president, I could say I want $7 million invested in this operation and they would go out and find $7 million."

Three years later, Middleton still bristled over an angry letter that outgoing university president Tim Wolfe wrote shifting the blame for the university's diversity problems to him. "You can hire someone for diversity, but without the resources you can't make any change. . . . You have to invest resources in what you want to do. It takes a lot more than giving someone a job and a title and ignoring them. . . . The president has to be the one to say this is what we're doing; this is what the university is about."

After fifteen months, Middleton was succeeded by Mun Y. Choi, the university's twenty-fourth, and first Asian American, president. Middleton left in place Kevin McDonald, the university's first chief diversity officer, who has degrees in law and psychology. "He has the academic pedigree. He has the pedagogy. He reports to the president. I wanted at the system level to have someone at the board meetings who could call them out. He's comfortable talking to the board of curators and also reports to the chancellor."

Even those who are encouraged by the academy's renewed engagement with diversity fear it is a fad that will fade, as it did by the 1980s when many of the gains made in the 1960s and 1970s were rolled back or erased. Middleton said this time he hopes colleges and universities will pay as much attention to retention as to hiring. "We need more people. We need universities to produce more PhDs from these underrepresented groups," he said, noting the dearth of junior faculty hired fresh out of doctoral programs.

To diversify their ranks, universities continue to recycle the same small number of faculty of color, leaving their overall number unchanged. "It's a systemic problem," Middleton said. "They [scholars of color] come here and enhance their credentials and six years later somebody's looking for them. We have to figure out a way to match the offers from other universities. We can't keep robbing every one of their people."

Middleton also noted the cultural isolation experienced by faculty of color at many universities, especially those outside of major cities. "They're the only one. People go to lunch with people they know and like. How do you make people gravitate toward people who don't look like them and have the same background? It's going to take decades of changing people's attitudes." He said while the pipeline remains an issue, "there's also opening that spigot and letting it flow" by giving recent graduates of color a chance. "White faculty are given a chance. Black and Latino faculty seldom get a lot of help. Nobody's going to allow for you to be less than perfect. You have to be really good at what you do and confident. People hire who they're comfortable with."

In 2018, Yale was again the focus of unwelcome news stories after a Black Yale student sleeping in a dormitory common room was reported to police by a White classmate. Yale president Salovey, in a campus-wide message, appealed to students, faculty, and staff to show greater sensitivity. "Each of us has the power to fight against prejudice and fear. I hope you will join me in doing so," he wrote.[17]

In an article for the *National Review*, Heather Mac Donald expressed outrage over Salovey's call for sensitivity and alleged that he "has chosen to fan the flames of racial grievance rather than to calm them."[18] She dismissed the incidence of racial profiling experienced by the Black student as "petty dormitory tyranny" and suggested that students of all races were confronted in equal measure by police. Left unspoken was the litany of minor encounters between police and people of color that end in fatalities or arrests.

The tendency to belittle Black grievance can be found across political persuasions. During a published debate with one of the 2015 Black Yale protesters, *Atlantic* magazine columnist Conor Friedersdorf appeared stumped by the student's expressed sense of oppression. "It would be easy," Friedersdorf wrote, "to know the way forward if the woes of students of color at Yale could be attributed to a Bull Connor heading up the administration, or Jim Crow-like policies segregating campus. Instead, as you note, the Yale community is basically 'opposed to the marginalization of people of color.' There is, however, disagreement about the best way forward."[19]

His words, however well intentioned, downplayed the inherent sense of alienation many Black students experience on campuses where their numbers are few and their culture and history are marginalized or outright demeaned. Moreover, he revealed the blind spot that many Whites, left and right, have when it comes to the ways of twenty-first-century bias. It no longer requires the hoses, tear gas, and dogs weaponized in Bull Connor's day. Videotaped scenes of brutalized civil rights protesters have been replaced by images of fleeing or handcuffed Blacks being shot or choked by police, often with impunity, along with the racial profiling and mass incarceration of Black and Brown men. Black students on college campuses are not hermetically sealed off from the larger world they inhabit; they experience the same racial profiling and stereotyping on campuses that they do in the larger world and know how easily they could become the next tragic subject of media headlines.

While racial customs and decorum in public settings have radically changed, the deep-seated prejudices many Whites hold of Black and Brown people have apparently not. A 2016 survey of two thousand non-Hispanic White Trump support-ers commissioned by *Slate* magazine found that 38 percent per-ceived Blacks as less human than Whites. Many used words like "savage" and "barbaric" or "lacking self-restraint, like animals" to describe African Americans. "White respondents routinely described Black people in dehumanizing ways," said the arti-cle. "Some examples: 'I consider Blacks to be closer to the ani-mal kingdom,' one respondent said, because Blacks 'lack the intelligence and morals' of other races. Another said that Black people 'carry and conduct themselves' in ways that are 'almost animalistic'"[20]

In 2007, six separate studies by Penn State researchers found that many Americans continue to link Blacks with apes and mon-keys, as they had in the early twentieth century when most scien-tists validated that view. "Not Yet Human: Implicit Knowledge, Historical Dehumanization and Contemporary Consequences," published in the February 2008 issue of the *American Psycho-logical Association's Journal of Personality and Social Psychology*, found that African Americans convicted of capital crimes were far more likely than their White counterparts to be described as "barbaric," "beast," "brute," or "savage" in hundreds of news sto-ries published in the *Philadelphia Inquirer* from 1979 to 1999.

These attitudes undoubtedly influence police interactions with Black and Brown people, who are often presumed to be crim-inally suspect. *Investigation of the Ferguson Police Department*, a one-hundred-page US Justice Department report released on March 4, 2015, found systemic racial bias practiced by Ferguson police and courts against its Black and poor citizens. Ferguson police were found to routinely engage in a pattern of stopping Blacks without reasonable suspicion and making arrests without probable cause, while courts were found to routinely impose undue penalties and jail time for minor offenses by Blacks. Ferguson police were found to be in violation of the First, Fourth, and Fourteenth Amendments. There's little reason to believe these abuses are unique to Ferguson.

However, when viewed in isolation, many Whites see Blacks' response to all but the most extreme cases of bias as overreaction. In 2009, an uproar ensued following the arrest of Harvard law professor Henry Louis Gates in his Cambridge, Massachusetts, home. Gates—among America's most prominent Black scholars—was incensed when officers appeared at his door asking him to step outside after a neighbor reported a possible burglary. The escalating tension resulted in the arrest of the bespectacled, fifty-eight-year-old professor. News of the episode went viral after the characteristically reserved President Obama, perhaps triggered by his own experiences while a student at Harvard Law School, said the arresting officers had behaved "stupidly." It would take what became known as a beer summit at the White House with Obama, Gates, and the police officer to defuse the controversy.

In 2018, a former Obama administration official was similarly confronted by police after a White neighbor reported a burglary as he was moving into his new Manhattan apartment. The same year, a seemingly endless string of episodes would at times take on comical proportions on social media, with Whites who called police on Blacks engaged in routine activities earning monikers such as "Barbeque Becky," "Cornerstore Caroline," or "Permit Patty." The common infraction by African Americans was satirized as "Walking While Black," "Driving While Black," or simply "Breathing While Black."

On May 29, 2018, Starbucks closed more than eight thousand stores in the United States for a "racial bias education day" for its 175,000 employees after a Philadelphia store manager called the police on two Black customers after one asked to use the restroom. The two Black men were arrested and handcuffed within minutes of entering the store, sparking complaints from customers who witnessed the incident. A video of the episode went viral, and days later Starbucks CEO Kevin Johnson met with the two men to personally apologize. The company called on some of the nation's most prominent civil rights leaders and reached out to faculty at Arizona State University to develop "an innovative open source curriculum to address specific forms of bias."

In June of 2019, the beauty retail chain Sephora closed more than four hundred stores for diversity training and launched its "We Belong to Something Beautiful" campaign after R & B singer SZA tweeted that she was racially profiled in a California store. The singer said she was shopping when an employee, suspecting her of stealing, called security.

It's doubtful that a one-day training session or open-source handbook can effectively address deeply entrenched and systemic racial bias, even if the gesture implies company contrition and resolve. While similar episodes of bias persist, these commonplace encounters don't typically make the news or result in ceremonious White House summits.

What for Whites are snapshots of seemingly minor encounters are for many people of color ceaseless drops of water that over time overflow into oceans of rage. And these episodes can prove deadly, as in the case of Sandra Bland, who was pulled over for a minor traffic infraction and ended up dead in her jail cell, or Botham Shem Jean, who in 2018 was shot and killed in his home by a Dallas police officer who claimed she thought he was an intruder and insisted he didn't obey commands.

Jennifer Eberhardt, a social psychologist, Stanford professor, and MacArthur Award recipient, has conducted a series of studies that show the impact of bias on law enforcement and that explain the routine nature of Whites suspecting Blacks of wrongdoing. Her studies consistently show that Whites more readily associate Blacks with crime and that Whites are more inclined to favor more punitive policies for Blacks. For example, in the 2014 study "Racial Disparities in Incarceration Increases Acceptance of Punitive Policies," she and her coauthor found when penal institutions were seen as "more Black," respondents were more concerned about crime and accepted more punitive policies than when the institution was "less Black."

"Exposure to extreme racial disparities, then, can lead people to support the very policies that produce those disparities, thus perpetuating a vicious cycle," the study said.[21] In other studies Eberhardt found that suspects with stereotypically African features have tougher jury verdicts, longer prison and death sentences, and a greater probability of mistaken identity. The problematic perception of Black barbarity, mirrored in mass media representations, becomes a self-fulfilling reality that serves to normalize the hyper-criminalization of Blacks in society and on college campuses.[22]

For students of color at most American colleges and universities, their cultural and racial isolation is set against the disproportionately White composition of the faculty, administrators, and students who are often inured to their cultural experience. So when students in educational environments are counseled to

learn to deal with adversity or, in the case of offensive Halloween costumes, "look away," they are left to believe that they, and
not the faculty, administrators, and their White peers, are solely
accountable for racial harmony. White students, in turn, become
proxies for societal norms.

Schools have long been the battleground on which issues of
race and social mobility have been waged. During the early years
of the twentieth century, leading patrons of education insisted
that Blacks pursue industrial education to prepare for subservi-
ent roles in society. That view was supported by *Negro Education: A Survey of the Private and Higher Schools for Colored People
in the United States*, an influential report authored by Thomas
Jesse Jones, a leading White educator, and published in 1916
by the US Education Bureau and the Phelps-Stokes Fund's
Education Commission. The report would influence the course
of African American education for decades and result in the
defunding of schools that offered Blacks a classical academic
curriculum. Based on a survey of 747 African American schools
in the South, the two-volume *Negro Education* concluded that
too many of the schools offered traditional courses in Latin, history, and mathematics that were irrelevant to the social reality
of African Americans. It proposed instead a model that stressed
manual and industrial education, with an emphasis on agriculture. The report coined the term "adaptive education" to describe
the type of instruction believed most applicable to the environment, social status, and ability of African Americans.

The report advocated instruction that "requires decreasing
emphasis on educational courses whose chief claim to recognition is founded on custom and tradition."[23]

Absurdly overlooking historical events such as slavery, legally mandated illiteracy, and racial hostility and rigid racial barriers that consistently undermined African American advancement, the report instead attributed the inferior social status of Blacks to their innate characteristics. "The high death rate of the colored people, their ignorance and disregard of simple physical laws, their perplexing economic and social status, establishes the claim of these subjects [sanitation, elementary science, history, and civics] to a large place in the curriculum of these schools."[24]

The report stressed that education for African Americans should be limited to training for manual skills, preposterously arguing "the Negro's highly emotional nature requires on balance as much as possible of the concrete and the definite."[25]

The report was assailed by eminent scholars W. E. B. Du Bois and Carter G. Woodson, the founder of *The Journal of Negro History*, who said it set African Americans back a generation. They had reason to be critical. The report would lead to the defunding of schools like Atlanta University, which offered Blacks classical academic training, and lead to the rise of manual training as the exclusive mode of instruction for Black students. Some schools, such as Booker T. Washington's Tuskegee Institute, which became the model for industrial education, continued to offer a classical academic curriculum to an elite cadre of students, but it did so covertly so as not to offend White patrons.[26]

Not until the 1954 *US Supreme Court Brown v. Board of Education* decision was school segregation deemed unconstitutional and parity across racial lines stamped into law. But in practice many schools, including colleges and universities, remained virtually segregated until the 1960s, when some lawmakers finally began to acknowledge that work needed to be done to address centuries of slavery, legalized discrimination, and stereotypes about Black aptitude. In 1961, President John F. Kennedy argued that federal contractors needed to take "affirmative action" to hire people without regard of their race, color, or religion. Then, in 1965, President Lyndon Johnson signed an executive order requiring government contractors to take "affirmative action" to increase the number of minorities and women, a policy that was adopted by schools. Since the 1960s, affirmative action programs have resulted in the number of minority college applicants doubling or tripling.

With the growing integration of students and faculty of color in the 1960s came demands for a more diverse curriculum that resulted in the establishment of Black studies programs, followed by others that sought to decenter the Eurocentric canon. These challenges inevitably resulted in the culture wars that continue to play out today.

While the percentage of Black and Latino students pursuing bachelor's degrees has gradually risen over the past five decades, White faculty, as noted earlier, continue to hold a disproportionate share—83 percent—of full-time professorships. Meanwhile, underrepresented minorities, particularly African Americans and Hispanics, are 4 percent and 3 percent, respectively, of full-time professors, with the fastest growth of faculty of color in non-tenure track positions.

Edna Chun, a higher education consultant and former university administrator, said that while Asian faculty are not recognized by most schools as underrepresented minorities, a disproportionate share of Asian faculty are not Asian Americans but foreign nationals, which gives a false sense of their overrepresentation. Moreover, she said Asian women, who are

3 percent of university professors, remain underrepresented in practically every academic discipline and are far less likely to secure tenure.[27]

A 2016 study by the Teachers Insurance and Annuity Institute found that a higher percentage of faculty of color are at two-year public and less selective institutions, rather than private, four-year private institutions. A study of administrators of color at major private universities found "token to modest" diversity in most senior positions. Administrators of color were disproportionately in diversity or student affairs positions.[28] Chun and Evans argue that the "continued dominance of White, male, heterosexual perspectives" in higher education administration "has failed to foster a representative bureaucracy that is responsive to the needs of diverse students."[29]

In sharp contrast to the impressions of student and faculty of color, a 2018 Gallup survey of college presidents representing 340 public and 262 private institutions found that 80 percent believed race relations on their campus were excellent or good. Whether the incongruence is due to delusion or their attempt to divert attention from persisting racial discord, their response negates the experiences of large numbers of students and faculty of color and indicates they see no need to change course. However, many presidents had a less positive view of relations on campuses elsewhere. Sixty-seven percent thought relations on campuses in general were fair. Sixty-nine percent feared Trump's rhetoric was adversely affecting the recruitment of international students, a concern likely influenced by the loss of tuition by international students who pay full freight. Only 30 percent strongly agreed that classrooms were as welcoming to conservative students as to liberal students. And 61 percent believed that public attention and policy related to diversity in higher education would recede, yet another indication that attention paid to diversity is tied more to headlines than an overriding commitment to social justice.

Richard Bribiescas became Yale's vice provost of diversity and development in January 2015, some nine months before the campus unrest. "In the academic community we live in a bubble. That bubble burst," he said.[30]

Three years after student protests shook Yale's bucolic campus, tensions had subsided but faculty diversity—one of the issues that had roiled the campus—remained unresolved. Bribiescas said while there had been some sixty-five appointments of faculty of color since 2015, the overall number of underrepresented faculty had slightly decreased due to low retention, one of the issues Middleton had raised at the University of Missouri. While the numbers were slightly down, between 2015 and 2017, the percentage of African American faculty remained largely unchanged, dipping from 3.4 percent to 3.38 percent; Hispanic faculty slightly increased from 3.38 percent to 3.76 percent, whereas Asian faculty slightly dipped, from 13.9 percent to 13.6 percent. However the "unknown" racial category expanded from 2.9 percent to 5.4 percent. One of the highest-profile departures was of Jonathan Holloway, the university's first African American college dean, who left to become the provost at Northwestern University.

Bribiescas attributes the university's low retention of faculty of color to the campus climate. "You have to feel you are wanted at the university," he said. In 2015, following the student uprising, Yale dedicated $50 million to faculty diversity. The amount appears substantial, but Bribiescas said that left $5 million annually to be expended across the university, an amount that he said "is right up there with recycling."

"You have to do more than appoint a diversity person," he said. "But that's been the strategy across academia."

Bribiescas, an anthropologist who had chaired the department at Yale, is especially attuned to concerns of students of color on campus, given his academic discipline and his own Mexican heritage. He recalls growing up in South Central Los Angeles when, as an eight-year-old child, he was pulled over by immigration authorities to question him about his parents' immigration status. Later, in the 1980s, he was a student activist at UCLA during protests over racial issues. "Fraternities would throw beer and tortillas at us. There was a culture of complacency. It's a common theme. Mistakes are repeated. It's one of the challenges across universities . . . It's endemic. We started to think we're leaving this behind, but it was just plastered over. Now, with social media, it's being documented. It's empowering."

Now that the matters have come to light, he said, universities need to put people committed to diversity in key leadership positions beyond positions such as his. At Yale, Bribiescas said being a senior person of color in the administration can at times be alienating and make his mission appear like a personal, as opposed to a university, priority. Among the other challenges for university presidents at legacy institutions such as Yale are alumni, who are overwhelmingly White and male and often less inclined to champion diversity.

"That is a challenge, but at some point you have to think it's the cost you're willing to bear to move the needle," Bribiescas said. "Sometimes you have to take a hit from the press and the alumni. You have to admit you have a problem, that the school has a problem. You're going to have to have a different conversation and accountability. What are the values of the university?"

He pointed to Drew Gilpin Faust, the first woman president at Harvard, as a stellar example, noting how she targeted the all-male study clubs. "That was bold, not reckless," he said. "We need to address racism and sexism. We benefitted from this, and now we have to turn the corner. There has to be a new generation of leadership."

Bribiescas said he was encouraged by the appointment of Weili Cheng as the executive director of the university alumni association. He believes she will encourage more alumni of color, and others who believe in the diversity mission, to reengage with the school. He is also inspired by Yale's long-term investment in scholars of color through its Presidential Visiting Fellows program that each year brings nine underrepresented scholars to campus. The university has also invested in the Dean's Emerging Scholars Initiative, which provides funding for fifteen doctoral students admitted under the initiative and an additional ten awarded through competitive research grants.

"The good news is that there are unbelievably dedicated, brilliant people working on this," he said. "They want to advance and attract the best and brightest. It's about priorities and values."[31]

But even those institutions that are committed to recruiting and retaining diverse faculty must consider how American college campuses have historically been inhospitable environments for people of color and determine what they might do to make them more inclusive.

CHAPTER

4

CIVIL WARS: LEGACY OF AN INGLORIOUS PAST

In 2018, in the midst of national debates over Confederate monuments, protesters tied a rope to a statue erected just over a century earlier on the University of North Carolina Chapel Hill campus and yanked it from its pedestal.

The toppled statue of *Silent Sam*, an anonymous Confederate soldier, incited glee but also days of outrage as protesters waving flags of the Lost Cause and signs imploring "Save our monuments" clashed with dissenters, culminating in assaults and arrests.

Across the country, similar skirmishes over an unreconciled past shattered campus civility as battle lines were drawn over whether racially divisive relics still had a prominent place on a modern-day campus. Unlike protests over campus climate, curriculum, and the lack of student and faculty diversity, these sought to expose universities' public expression of ideals through their prominent public iconography.

At Harvard Law School, as previously indicated, students demanded the removal of a school crest, while at Washington and Lee University, school officials grappled with the legacy of Confederate general Robert E. Lee, one of the school's namesakes, whose image is ubiquitous across the campus. At Princeton University, the student-formed Black Justice League called for the removal of Woodrow Wilson's mural from a dining hall and his name from the School of Public and International Affairs and a residential college. The students cited his position against school integration during his tenure as university president and his segregation of the federal workforce while US president. At the University of Texas, several Confederate statues, including one of President Jefferson Davis, were relocated from outdoor spaces on campus to a museum.

In 2017 protesters carrying tiki torches and Confederate flags marched through the University of Virginia campus protesting plans to remove a statue of Robert E. Lee from a public park. The Universities Studying Slavery consortium, a network of more than fifty colleges and universities seeking to navigate the minefield of iconography and history, had been launched on the campus three years earlier.

But these debates over iconography detract from the even more unsettling ways in which America's colleges and universities are implicated in the nation's racial strife. Far from being neutral bystanders of our vexed history, they were the chief architects and custodians of a meticulously crafted system that lies at the heart of recurring chaos.

Many institutions of higher education were not only beneficiaries of slavery, they were also home to the influential authors
and proselytizers of specious pseudo-scientific racial theories
that rationalized and sustained it. Well into the twentieth century, an ideology of European supremacy and African inferiority,
embedded in the canon, prevailed at most institutions of higher
learning, including Harvard, Princeton, Yale, and Columbia.
These ideas, hardwired into the American ethos, continue to
pervert the nation's ideals and thwart its progress. Efforts to
diversify classrooms and workplaces are left to compete with
this dangerously flawed, and insufficiently contested, history.

Whole disciplines were rooted in ideas of European superiority and the notion that they stood at the pinnacle of civilization and Africans at the nadir. As I recounted in my previous
book *Spectacle: The Astonishing Life of Ota Benga*, Louis Agas-
siz, the Harvard professor who at the time of his death in 1873
was arguably America's most venerated scientist, had for more
than two decades insisted that Blacks were a separate species, a
"degraded and degenerate race."

In his outgoing address as president of the American Association for the Advancement of Science, University of Pennsylvania professor Daniel Garrison Brinton asserted that races
are not equally endowed. "The black, the brown, and the red
races differ anatomically so much from the white, especially in
their splanchnic organs, that even with equal cerebral capacity
they never could rival its results by equal efforts," he said in an
address memorialized in the November 1895 edition of *Popular
Science* magazine.[1] He dismissed claims by some that historical
events and social barriers, and not biology, accounted for the

disparity in achievement between races. These ideas seamlessly flowed into the twentieth century.

In *The Basis of Social Relations: A Study in Ethnic Psychology*, posthumously published in 1902 by G. P. Putnam's Sons in New York and London as part of the Webster Collection of Social Anthropology, and in other writing, Brinton asserted that Africans are "midway between the Oran-utang [*sic*] and the European white."[2] This ideology, then, sanctioned by a major publisher and stamped into an iconic and authoritative reference book, would serve to inform a generation of American scholars.

Henry Fairfield Osborn, a Princeton graduate who was among his era's most esteemed scientists, was an ardent eugenicist who in 1921, while president of the American Museum of Natural History, hosted the Second International Congress of Eugenics there, with Alexander Graham Bell serving as honorary president.[3] The group was a major proponent of some of the proposed policies that in the 1920s became law, including the Immigration Restriction Act, which sought to address the rise of immigration from Asia and eastern and southern Europe; the Virginia Racial Integrity Act, which banned marriages between Whites and non-Whites; and Virginia's Eugenical Sterilization Act, which permitted the sterilization of asylum inmates who were epileptic, severely disabled, or "feeble-minded." Osborn would also host and serve as honorary president of the third and final congress at the museum in 1932.

He penned the introduction to *The Passing of the Great Race*, an influential book that advocated the cleansing of "inferior races" from the United States through birth control, racial segregation, and anti-miscegenation and anti-immigration laws. In it, the author, Madison Grant, infamously wrote:

> Whether we like to admit it or not, the result of the mixture of two races, in the long run, gives us a race reverting to the more ancient, generalized and lower type. The cross between a white man and an Indian is an Indian; the cross between a white man and a negro is a negro; the cross between a white man and a Hindu is a Hindu; and the cross between any of the three European races and a Jew is a Jew.[4]

Praise for the book was nearly universal. President Theodore Roosevelt called it "a capital book—in purpose, in vision, in grasp of the facts," and Hitler called it his "Bible."[5]

While by the 1960s many of these theories were debunked, most colleges and universities have yet to forthrightly confront their lineage and legacy. This troubling ideology still finds expression in film, literature, news media, advertising, and fashion and is most pronounced in our courts and prisons. The deafening silence has enabled many—from scholars at prestigious universities to media pundits—to continue to claim that factors other than history and remaining institutional barriers account for persistent economic, health, and other disparities along racial lines.[6]

In *Ebony and Ivy*, historian Craig Steven Wilder vividly recounts how the academy is implicated in the subjugation of Africans and Native Americans to facilitate the financing, construction, and expansion of the university system and the fabrication of an ideology of White supremacy. "Race did not come from science and theology; it came to science and theology.

Science and theology deferred to race, twisting and warping under the weight of an increasingly popular and sweeping understanding of human affairs that tied the social fates of different populations to perceived natural capacities."[7]

Illustrating how the slave trade funded the rise of the earliest American colleges and universities in the colonies, he recounts how Rev. George Berkeley became a patron of Yale, to which he contributed his ninety-six-acre slave plantation in Rhode Island. Rent secured from slave-owning tenants was used to sponsor university scholarships.

In New York, many of the trustees of King's College, which would become Columbia University, were slave traders, and during its first two decades, the school "enrolled more children of Atlantic traders than any other college in British North America," Wilder writes.[8] Philip Livingston, one of its founding benefactors, was among the city's most prominent slaveholding and slave-trading families and had inherited enslaved people and commercial slaving interests from his parents and in-laws. Similarly, founding trustees of the College of Philadelphia, which became the University of Pennsylvania, invested in enslaved Africans from the Caribbean and indentured servants from Europe. They advertised for runaways and from their offices sold enslaved people. Philadelphia mayor Charles Willing, another charter trustee, owned three ships and led at least six slave expeditions. "Prominent families such as the Allens, Turners, and Whartons shaped the iron industry, which used enslaved black and indentured white labor," Wilder wrote.[9] And the College of New Jersey, which became Princeton, boasted a large proportion of slaveholding families, many recruited from the South, and the school "was among the most welcoming places in the northern colonies to the sons of planters."[10] The governor of New Hampshire lured Rev. Eleazar Wheelock to establish Dartmouth College, where the enslaved on campus outnumbered faculty, administrators, and active trustees and rivaled its number of students.[11]

Nicholas Boyston, a Boston merchant responsible for one of Harvard's first endowed chairs, had also been enriched by his family's involvement in the slave trade, as was Thomas Hubbard, a 1721 Harvard graduate who for more than two decades served as the university's treasurer. For two hundred years, Harvard's history, Wilder wrote, "was inseparable from the history of slavery and the slave trade."

These colleges not only trained the men who would lead the colonies but also provided the rationale for the enslavement of Africans and the brutal removal of Native Americans.

"Modern slavery required the acquiescence of scholars and the cooperation of academic institutions," Wilder wrote.[12]

The benefits to these institutions and their graduates did not end with the demise of the slave trade or the end of slavery. Wilder notes how for centuries college graduates apprenticed under slave traders from New England, the Mid-Atlantic, and Europe before migrating to the South and West Indies to work as doctors, merchants, teachers, ministers, lawyers, and politicians.

"The academy never stood apart from American slavery," Wilder concluded. "In fact, it stood beside church and state as the third pillar of a civilization built on bondage."[13]

But if acquiescence to racist ideology was required for colleges and universities to flourish in the past, to what do these institutions owe their adherence to the suppression and sanitizing of history and the maintenance of divisive iconography today?

In 2015 the UNC system chancellor commissioned a history task force to determine how to curate the campus iconography and teach the history of the university. The campus unrest threatened to mirror August 2017 protests in Charlottesville over plans to remove a statue of Robert E. Lee from a public park. The decision by the city council had sparked protests by Unite the Right, a group of White supremacists who marched through the University of Virginia campus. Their protests drew counter-protesters, including Heather Heyer, a thirty-two-year-old paralegal who was killed when James Alex Fields Jr. drove his vehicle into the crowd, injuring twenty-eight people. He was convicted of first-degree murder and malicious wounding, among other charges.

"August 2017 was a wakeup call for White Americans who have not really confronted this history and how being White has privileged them and how communities have shaped their public memory," said Kirt von Daacke, a history professor and assistant dean at UVA who chaired its President's Commission on Slavery and the University.[14] "Charlottesville is known as a White progressive place, but there's a pretty unpleasant story dealing with slavery and segregation. What we're wrestling with is a microcosm of what America has not come to terms with since the Civil Rights Movement. It so powerfully shapes the world we're in."

The UNC task force was set up with the express purpose of addressing the same history that was reverberating during the Charlottesville rally. "It's kind of a reckoning with the past," said Cecelia Moore, the UNC historian and member of its history task force. "We're not done yet."[15]

Their first order of business was addressing student demands to rename Saunders Hall, named for William Saunders, a former Ku Klux Klan leader. The group moved to remove his name and install an exhibit in the building that told the larger story of UNC, North Carolina, and the history of Reconstruction and segregation.

The second project entailed studying the signs and history around McCorkle Place, the historic quad where *Silent Sam* had stood. But in 2018, the issue over the statue's fate was tied up in legal battles. Thom Goolsby, a former state senator and member of the university system's statewide board of governors, insisted that the monument should be remounted "without delay." He cited a state law passed in 2015 that restricts the removal and relocation of monuments on public property and set a ninety-day deadline to replace those that had been temporarily removed.

However, in a letter to the UNC system, Gov. Roy Cooper argued that the law allows officials to do what's necessary to avoid "threats to public safety."[16] In December, the university presented its proposal to the governing board that reports directly to the state legislature. The task force recommended removing the tablets and other racially fraught iconography and contextualizing it, along with the statue, at a new center for education and history to be constructed by 2022. The new building was estimated to cost $5.3 million, with an additional $800,000 in annual operating costs. However, the board of governors rejected UNC-Chapel Hill's plan and recommended the formation of a committee to devise a new and less costly plan.

In the meantime, *Silent Sam*, erected in 1913 to honor alumni who "answered the call," is not on view. The base on which it was mounted and the tablets honoring the Confederacy were finally removed in January 2019. "The monument's not gone until it's all gone," Moore said. "It's not honoring soldiers who died in war but a cause, and reminds future generations to answer the call to duty. . . . I'm a historian. In terms of eras, this is still fairly recent history. Legal segregation only ended thirty years ago. To think we were done was a bit naïve."[17]

UNC is among the more than fifty colleges and universities from across the country that are members of the Universities Studying Slavery consortium that meets twice a year to exchange scholarship and consider proposals for change. "It's about a truth-telling mission," said von Daacke, one of the founding members of what began as an informal gathering of Virginia schools. "It's hard to do when you're home alone," he added, noting that schools are often hesitant to dredge up their role in the nation's shameful past out of fear of stigma.[18] However, he said that with the exception of a handful of schools, such as Oberlin and Berea Colleges, every school from that era has a similarly shameful past. "Our contribution is encouraging other schools, sharing best practices," he said.

The group is seeking, among other things, sustainable ways to both honor and confront the past. Von Daacke said romanticized narratives about the Civil War are the most difficult to dismantle. "We can talk about slavery. People can compartmentalize it as something that happened a long time ago. Slavery and the racism it was intertwined with—they don't see it today. . . . We're in a moment of acknowledging it was a crime and it was wrong. But we are not ready to talk about the memory of the Civil War.

How we remember the Civil War and the Confederacy, you run into some pretty steep headwinds."

Many, he said, continue to cling to mythology, including the claim that Robert E. Lee actually freed the enslaved. He said these "Lost Cause" adherents continue to appear at the shrouded Lee statue to remove the tarp. "I don't know how we get rid of that," he said. "They're immune to reason and evidence."

While many of the battles over iconography play out in the South, the history of slavery has less well-known roots in the North. At Harvard Law, the dean appointed a committee of faculty, students, alumni, and staff to consider the crest adopted by the school in 1937 in recognition of Isaac Royall Jr. Royall not only acquired his wealth from the trade and labor of enslaved Africans but had allegedly murdered some of them. In 2016, the committee recommended the retirement of the crest that had adorned buildings, the school stationery, and diplomas. Emblazoned across it was "*Veritas*," Latin for truth, the school motto. The recommendation to remove the crest was supported by the university and approved by the Harvard Corporation, its governing board.

"We cannot choose our history but we can choose that for which we stand," read a statement from Martha Minow, the law school dean. "Above all, we rededicate ourselves to the hard work of eradicating not just symbols of injustice but injustice itself."[19] Wrote then-university president Drew Gilpin Faust and senior fellow William F. Lee: "The school will actively explore other steps to recognize rather than to suppress the realities of its history, mindful of our shared obligation to honor the past not by seeking to erase it, but rather by bringing it to light and learning from it."[20]

At Princeton, however, the Trustee Committee on Woodrow Wilson's Legacy voted against the removal of Wilson's name from the school. Its report said: "Wilson, like other historical figures, leaves behind a complex legacy with both positive and negative repercussions, and the use of his name implies no endorsement of views and actions that conflict with the values and aspirations of our times." Instead, it recommended a recommitment to diversity and the establishment of a pipeline program to increase the number of underrepresented minorities among the ranks of faculty, graduate students and postdocs. It also recommended efforts to diversify campus art and iconography and to promote greater transparency about Princeton's historical legacy.

In response, the Black Justice League issued a blistering statement that read in part: "Princeton remains unable to even reckon and wrestle with its white supremacist foundations and its ongoing role in perpetuating racism." It said the decision "demonstrates unambiguously its commitment to symbols and legacies of anti-Blackness in the name of 'history' and 'tradition' at the expense of the needs of and in direct contravention with the daily experiences of Black students at Princeton."[21]

The students continued to call for the removal of the Woodrow Wilson mural from a dining hall, cultural competency training for faculty and staff, amended curriculum requirements to incorporate issues around diversity and marginalization, and the creation of "a Black cultural space." In 2013, a Princeton Trustee Ad Hoc Committee on Diversity had, among other things, recommended unconscious bias training, regular climate surveys, and focus groups "designed to capture a diversity of voices." The committee issued a statement that read: "In the face of insufficient progress and with compelling reasons to move forward, the Committee believes that Princeton must renew its commitment to diversity with a sense of urgency."[22]

The protests at Harvard and Princeton shed light on a history that has long been suppressed and unspoken. While the South has for decades publicly confronted its racial transgressions, elite northern institutions have seldom been made to account for their ties to slavery and the ways in which they legitimized and maintained racial ideologies that continue to resonate today.

At Washington and Lee, whose namesakes are George Washington and Robert E. Lee, the issue of Confederate iconography took on heightened significance. Following the violent clashes in Charlottesville, Washington and Lee president Will Dudley felt compelled to respond. Noting the school's "complex history," he said that Lee, whose statue had provoked "these hateful groups," had become a particularly polarizing symbol. "This gives us a special obligation to be absolutely clear about what we stand for as an institution," he said.[23] In August 2017, he empaneled a commission "to lead us in an examination of how our history—and the ways that we teach, discuss, and represent it—shapes our community."[24] A less formal Working Group on the History of African Americans at W&L had previously been formed.

Lee's name is but a portion of the school's fraught history. Until 1852, it had enslaved and sold Africans to finance its growth. But Lee's presence pervades the leafy campus. In addition to the prominent statue of him on his horse at the entrance, his portrait is ubiquitous, and his name is on Lee House, the president's residence, and the chapel museum. Inside the chapel rests a marble statue of him, and beneath it his remains and those of his family are contained in an underground mausoleum.

In May 2018, the university Commission on Institutional History and Community issued its report, which recommended ways to change the school's visual culture to create a more inclusive environment. The report noted how Lee imagery across the campus depicted him as chivalrous and saintly. "By continuing to hold rituals and events in Lee Chapel," it said, "the university, wittingly or not, sustains the Shrine of the South and the memory of Lee as a commander of the Confederate Army."[25]

In response, the university moved to retain Lee's name on the chapel and president's house and to rename a hall in recognition of John Chavis, an African American who had graduated from what was then Washington Academy in 1799. The university also renamed Lee-Jackson House for Pamela Hemenway Simpson, the first tenured female professor at the university, who had helped Washington and Lee University to transition to a coeducational school. The university is also hiring a director of institutional history, who will be tasked with telling the fuller story of the school's difficult history.

This was not the first time the university had attempted to address its past. In 2014, Black law school students had requested that the school contextualize the monuments and Confederate flags that appeared to celebrate the Confederacy and to cease allowing neo-Confederates to march on campus on Lee-Jackson Day.

Then-president Kenneth Ruscio pledged to address the issue. "Acknowledging that historical record—and acknowledging the contributions of those individuals—will require coming to terms with a part of our past that we wish had been different but that we cannot ignore," he said. "We are committed to telling the university's history accurately, including the stories of many individuals who should not be overlooked."[26]

Brown University was perhaps the first to publicly acknowledge its ties to slavery when in 2003 then-president Ruth Simmons, who is African American, appointed a Steering Committee on Slavery and Justice. "We cannot change the past," said the committee's final report. "But an institution can hold itself accountable for the past, accepting its burdens and responsibilities along with its benefits and privileges. This principle applies particularly to universities, which profess values of historical continuity, truth seeking and service."[27] Among its recommendations was an annual day of remembrance, a rewriting of the school's history, public forums, and discussions of the university's historical relationship to slavery at freshman orientation. The school's Center for the Study, an interdisciplinary scholarly research center that hosts events and exhibitions, of Slavery and Justice grew out of the study.

"We're late to the party," said von Daacke, who traces the beginning of UVA's reckoning with its history to 2007 when, during the four hundredth anniversary celebration of the founding of Jamestown, the Virginia Assembly issued a statement of "profound regret" for its role in the enslavement of African people.[28] The university installed a plaque recognizing the thousands of unsung enslaved laborers who built and maintained the campus between 1817 and 1865. However, several years later, students protested the inadequacy of the plaque, which still managed to honor Thomas Jefferson's vision for the campus.

In 2013, UVA president Teresa A. Sullivan appointed a Commission on Slavery and the University, following the model established by Brown ten years before. "We went about our work—the institution had unleashed this process but wasn't comfortable embracing it publicly," von Daacke said. Over the course of the commission's five-year life, it began establishing a relationship with the region's African American community. "We didn't have a relationship [before that]," von Daacke said. "The community said the first thing you need to do is clean your own house. Be honest about your history and tell your own story. There's a lot more to do."

One of the commission's recommendations that has been embraced by the school is a monument to enslaved African Americans that will be displayed in a prominent place on campus by 2020. "That memorial is something the community wanted—to change the physical landscape to honor the past and the people who suffered through that," explained von Daacke. "We have lots of Civil War monuments and dubious monuments to the conquering of the West, but what we don't have are monuments to all the other people. They really do matter."

Rather than simple matters of justice, these interventions express the institutions' ideals and suggest the values they hope to impart to students.

Institutions cannot hope to achieve true diversity without meaningfully addressing the ways in which their own history so palpably informs the present. The debates over iconography are less about anachronistic relics than they are about the values and ideals they—and the institutions that flaunt them—express today.

CHAPTER

5

COURSE CORRECTION

I f ever the state of diversity at Columbia University College of Dental Medicine was alarmingly conspicuous, it was in 2002 when the incoming class of seventy-five students included just one underrepresented minority. Dr. Dennis Mitchell, a dental school assistant professor and, at the time, the director of the college's Harlem Community DentCare Network, said the lone student set the school's diversity deficit in stark relief. Then-dean Ira Lamster asked him to serve as senior associate dean for diversity affairs and to tackle the problem of what Mitchell called the "lonely only." Mitchell immediately set about designing a pilot pipeline program with the medical school funded by the Robert Wood Johnson Foundation. Within six years, the percentage of underrepresented minorities at the college increased sevenfold, from 3 percent to 21 percent. And contrary to the prediction of naysayers, the college remained within the top three in the country for the quantitative scores of incoming students.

"You need intention and leadership," said Mitchell, who in 2014, in addition to his role as senior associate dean for diversity affairs at the college, became vice provost for faculty advancement across the university. "It's not going to happen by mistake."[1]

Mitchell brought to his university-wide position a sense of history and appreciation for what had transpired a half century earlier in the wake of the Civil Rights Movement.

"I came from an era when you could be born in the Polo Grounds and get into a decent university," Mitchell said, referring to the economically tenuous area in Harlem that once housed a sports stadium. "You could be Colin Powell," he said of the former secretary of state born in Harlem to Jamaican immigrants who graduated from the public City College.

Today, he said, that's more difficult to do. "The public education system is such that many are not qualified to succeed. That changed in our lifetime. We've criminalized people of color. We've been rolling back most of what's been put in place. We're leaving so much of our population behind."

By the end of the 1970s, affirmative action—which had begun to close the racial gap in income and education—had given way to cries of reverse discrimination. In 1978, in *Bakke v. Regents of the University of California*, the US Supreme Court narrowly ruled in favor of Allan Bakke, a White student who sued the University of California Davis School of Medicine after he was twice denied admission. He blamed a program in which the school reserved sixteen out of one hundred seats for racial minorities. In a five-to-four decision, the US Supreme Court struck down the use of racial quotas in college admissions, saying they violated the Fourteenth Amendment's Equal Protection Clause. Writing for the majority, Supreme Court justice

Lewis F. Powell said it was unfair to impose the burden of history on the innocent, alluding to Bakke. The ruling meant that past discrimination of disadvantaged groups could not be used to justify discrimination in admission decisions. The burden of history, then, would not be shared but shouldered by the victims of legally prescribed discrimination and its legacy. The decision seemed to wipe the slate clean, as if history was unrelated to contemporary realities, and suggested that all members of society now operated on a level playing field. In his dissent, Justice Harry Blackmun asserted: "In order to get beyond racism we have to take account of race. There is no other way . . . in order to treat some persons equally, we must treat them differently."[2] Justice Thurgood Marshall, the first African American to sit on the Supreme Court, argued that the UC-Davis program was constitutional given the nation's racial history and the current status of Blacks in America, which he called "a tragedy."[3]

"It must be remembered that, during most of the past 200 years, the Constitution as interpreted by this Court did not prohibit the most ingenious and pervasive forms of discrimination against the Negro," he said. "Now, when a state acts to remedy the effects of that legacy of discrimination, I cannot believe that this same Constitution stands as a barrier."[4]

While quotas were deemed unconstitutional, diversity was viewed as a compelling state interest that enriched the overall college environment. Colleges could still consider race as one of myriad factors in admissions decisions.

The Bakke decision was followed in 1981 by the dismantlement of federal antidiscrimination programs under the Reagan administration. Affirmative action continued to be denigrated even after quotas were eliminated. By the 1980s, many of the gains made during the 1960s, including school integration, had been erased, along with federal policies that had begun to effectively close the education and poverty gap without Whites losing ground.

Today, while strategies used by colleges and universities to fill the relatively small number of spaces in the most selective schools are challenged in court, millions of Black and Brown children are condemned to overcrowded, underfunded schools in neighborhoods that Great Society programs were attempting, with some success, to address.

Lee Bollinger, a renowned First Amendment scholar, became the nineteenth president of Columbia University in 2002. He had previously served in the same role at the University of Michigan, where he had sharpened his sword for the conflicts ahead. The battle lines were already being drawn as he was installed as the twelfth president of the University of Michigan in February 1997. On October 14 of that year, Jennifer Gratz, a White student who two years earlier had been denied admission to the University of Michigan College of Literature, Science, and the Arts, served papers on the university. In *Gratz v. Bollinger*, she claimed that she was denied admission due to reverse discrimination. The university countered that its criteria, which considered race along with other factors, including geography, legacy, and athletic ability, fostered a diverse student body. A second lawsuit, *Grutter v. Bollinger*, was filed against the university on December 3, 1997. In it Barbara Grutter, another White student, also claimed reverse discrimination accounted for her being denied admission to the law school.

"I'm not sure I thought I'd be in this fight," Bollinger said during an interview at his university residence in 2018. However, beginning in the 1980s and throughout his five-year tenure as president of the University of Michigan, "a wave of antipathy landed at my doorstep. It kept growing," he said of attacks on affirmative action.[5]

In 1996, in *Hopwood v. Texas*, the US Court of Appeals ruled that race could not be a factor in admissions; the state of Texas appealed the decision to the Supreme Court, which refused to hear the case. Then, in *Johnson v. Regents of the University System of Georgia*, the US Court of Appeals determined that the use of race in admissions—in this case the assignment of points to non-White applicants—violated the Equal Protection Clause.

These attacks had an immediate effect on the diversity of colleges' student body. After California's passage in 1996 of Proposition 209, which abolished affirmative action programs in state hiring, contracting, and college admissions, underrepresented minority admissions plummeted 55 percent at UC Berkeley and UCLA. Similarly, the percentage of minority students in Rice University's freshman class dropped 32 percent after Texas eliminated affirmative action programs.

Nearly two decades later, in *Fisher v. University of Texas*, the Supreme Court was once again asked to intervene in race-based admission policies after Abigail Fisher, a White student, sued after she was denied admission. In its defense, the university cited a 2002 study showing that 79 percent of university courses had one or no African Americans enrolled, and 30 percent had one or no Hispanics. In 2013, the Supreme Court upheld the university's use of race but cited a standard of "strict scrutiny" that requires the university to prove to the court that race-neutral policies were attempted. Justice Anthony Kennedy, writing the majority opinion, said: "A university must make a showing that its plan is narrowly tailored to achieve the only interest that this Court has approved in this context: the benefits of a student body diversity that encompasses a . . . broad array of qualifications and characteristics of which racial or ethnic origin is but a single though important element."[6]

Bollinger had come of age during the civil rights era of the 1960s and 1970s and was not prepared to reverse course. He saw *Brown v. Board of Education* as a pivotal moment in the nation. "No matter what your field, *Brown v. Board* reshaped everything," he said. "When I saw that being attacked and undermined, that would be a trigger. So much of the way the society defines what it means to be in a just society was shaped in that era."[7]

Faced with the decision of settling the lawsuits against the University of Michigan or fighting, he chose to defend affirmative action as moral and just. "I decided we would fight this to the end. This would be the centerpiece of my six-year tenure there."

In 2003, a year after he became president of Columbia University, the US Supreme Court issued decisions for both affirmative action cases at the University of Michigan. In *Gratz v. Bollinger*, the court deemed as unconstitutional the University of Michigan's use of a point system—which accorded twenty points to underrepresented minorities. The majority again cited the Equal Protection Clause of the Fourteenth Amendment. However, that same year, in *Grutter v. Bollinger*, in a five-to-four decision, the Supreme Court upheld the admission policies of the University of Michigan Law School, a major victory that affirmed diversity as a compelling interest in college admissions.

The Grutter decision may have been a positive step, but it didn't give universities the power to recapture the progress made in the sixties and seventies. Bollinger said diversity has become an abstract concept due to the US Supreme Court's 1978 Bakke decision, which restricts remedies for past discrimination. It is precisely that history—the centuries of slavery followed by decades of legal and extra-legal discrimination—that affirmative action policies crafted in the 1960s attempted to repair. Without that rationale, African Americans are expected to compete on a playing field that has systematically been rigged against them.

"We're deprived of the context that gave it a sense of mission," Bollinger said, alluding to the Bakke decision. "Every college leader is told 'Do not refer to history.' I think we have a meaningless, abstract conversation about diversity without a rationale."

Given the legacy of slavery and legal discrimination marked by "massive disadvantages" for African Americans and "massive advantages" for White Americans, Bollinger said, "You have to believe in a principal of justice. There hasn't been enough pushback on the abstraction of diversity. You have to make it front and center. I think it's a matter of intention. If it's a pipeline issue, you have to work on the pipeline. The entire institution has to be behind it. Left to its own devices, it won't happen."[8]

In 2005, three years after arriving from the University of Michigan, Bollinger touted diversity as one of Columbia

University's core missions. He announced an $85 million initiative for faculty diversity recruitment and retention. His initiative would bring the issue to the forefront of university life and precede by a decade the activism that swept like wildfire across American campuses. Between 2007 and 2017, the percentage of underrepresented minorities on the tenure-track faculty expanded from 6.7 percent to 9.6 percent. The greatest gains were in the humanities (7.3 to 11 percent) and social sciences (7.9 to 12.7), and the least was in the natural sciences, where the numbers barely budged from 4.9 percent to 5.6 percent. The percentage of doctoral students grew from 10.4 percent to 15.4 percent.[9]

During fall 2017, Columbia announced an additional $100 million for its faculty diversity initiative. Mitchell, who by then was in the university-wide role of vice provost for faculty diversity and inclusion, described it as incentive based—"no stick, all carrot." Departments compete for target-of-opportunity faculty lines that allow them to recruit leading scholars from underrepresented groups to teach at the school. Resources range from $125,000 annually for non-lab-based lines to $250,000 for lab-based lines. Mitchell said while the incentives are great, the university does not penalize programs that choose not to participate. "We're in a competitive environment where people love to compete," Mitchell said. "We're very intentional about outcomes; the work."[10]

However, a 2018 equity report on the university diversity initiatives concluded that the target-of-opportunity hiring was having "a discouraging effect" on the program's potential. The equity report was the conclusion of a study that sought to understand why, given the university commitment, progress in diversity hiring had not been greater.[11] Because the targeted lines are funded for only three years, with costs thereafter absorbed by the departments, some faculty contend that the target-of-opportunity appointments compete with other programmatic priorities. The report recommended that diversity hiring become part of the mainstream "and not be seen as something departments do only for target of opportunity hires."

Unfortunately, measures such as targeted diversity hiring were created precisely because diverse faculty was not being realized through the normal process. The reasons for this are deeply entrenched. At colleges and universities, the faculty search process is typically run by a committee appointed by the chair of the department in question. That committee generally has wide latitude to reach out to anyone it deems suitable or desirable to join the faculty. Hiring, then, is a subjective process, and candidate finalists typically mirror the networks of those leading the search. Searches often result in the hiring of friends and former colleagues or of people whose backgrounds, scholarly interests, and sensibilities mirror those of the committee members. The candidates, then, tend to reflect the overwhelmingly White composition of the faculty. Add to this process of self-referential decision making the network of influential people who are then asked to write letters of recommendation, which leaves all but a small number of racial minorities out of the loop. For junior-level prospective candidates whose scholarship challenges White norms and views embedded in Euro-centered canons, the odds are especially long.

While at some schools faculty appointed through targeted hiring are a bonus, at Columbia they are "substitutional" rather than "incremental," which means they must be factored into a budget that does not allow for faculty growth. Bollinger pushed back on the notion that diversity can't be achieved without expanding the faculty.

"If we're a faculty of fifty faculty members, the fact that we're not growing to fifty-five does not mean that we can't become more diverse in our hiring in the next decade," he told the student-run *Columbia Spectator*. "I don't accept the proposition."[12]

Some accrediting bodies, like the Accrediting Council on Education in Journalism and Mass Communication (ACEJMC), have nudged schools to embrace diversity by considering it as part of a holistic assessment of journalism programs. To be accredited, a school is required to demonstrate that it has "an inclusive program that values domestic and global diversity, and serves and reflects society."[13]

Diversity and inclusiveness are among nine standards the council reviews every six years. (Others include student services, assessment of learning outcomes, and curriculum and instruction.) Programs that do not meet the council's requirements can receive provisional accreditation to give them time to address outstanding issues or be denied accreditation altogether, which can affect a school's reputation and outside funding. To pass the council's diversity and inclusion standard, a program must have a written plan "for achieving an inclusive curriculum, a diverse faculty and student population, and a supportive climate for working and learning and for assessing progress toward achievement of the plan."[14] In addition to an exhaustive review of curricula, programming, and recruitment and hiring numbers, a team of reviewers descend on the school for up to a week to conduct extensive interviews with faculty, administrators, and students. The onerous process, which requires faculties to compile extensive documentation, triggered a debate among some in journalism programs over whether having accreditation was worth the effort.

The debate intensified after Northwestern's highly regarded Medill School of Journalism decided to forgo the process. Columbia University, which houses the Pulitzer Prizes and is among the most prestigious journalism programs in the world, remained among the 112 journalism programs accredited by ACEJMC. Another five had provisional status. Left unsaid during the debate is whether accrediting bodies such as the ACEJMC have effectively pushed faculties that otherwise might not have made diversity a priority.

In addition to holding schools accountable, ACEJMC provides guidance on how to achieve diversity. A "diversity tip sheet" posted on its website leads with a quote from Jerry Ceppos, the former dean of the LSU Manship School of Mass Communication, which reads, "Diversifying faculty, students and curriculum is not rocket science . . . It's easy to diversify, especially if the message from the former dean, director or chair is unambiguous." The tip sheet advises: "If the pool isn't diverse, tell the committee to bring in one more candidate—the person of color who ranked highest on the list."[15]

It also suggests identifying outstanding underrepresented scholars and bringing them to the provost's attention even when there is not an opening.

"On one recent accreditation site team visit, the dean said no such incentives were available," the council reported on its website. "The team challenged the provost who said that he would be happy to consider adding a line for a diverse candidate."[16]

While it's not rocket science, these strategies may not be known to faculty members, who have continued to follow normal hiring protocols that consistently bear the same results. But even well-intentioned initiatives, like targeted hiring, can provoke resentment and speculation that a two-tiered system means that the bar has been lowered to attract underrepresented scholars, even when they are otherwise overlooked. Bribiescas has heard this view expressed at Yale, where he notes that, to some, diversity is anathema to excellence. He said that some of his White colleagues myopically undervalue scholarship and worldviews different from their own.

While faculty brought in under such initiatives can be stigmatized, faculties have also found ways to pervert the process by appealing for target-of-opportunity lines in instances when during a regular search a candidate of color is rated higher than are the White candidates. In those instances, the candidate of color—rather than being hired through the regular process—is proposed to the provost as a target of opportunity to enable the faculty to also hire the White candidate. In those instances, diversity is used as a cover to hire a White candidate who would otherwise not have gotten the job. While on the surface, this is a seemingly innocuous act, it neutralizes the diverse hire and subverts the spirit of an initiative intended to promote diversity by advantaging the already advantaged.

Moreover, once schools do prioritize diversity, many attempt to recruit the same cadre of proven stars in their fields while overlooking emerging scholars of color in the pipeline. As a result, the same superstars of color are recycled and move between schools, while the overall number of underrepresented faculty remains unchanged. The bidding wars over a relative handful of star faculty further incites resentment among some White faculty and perpetuates the sense that racial minorities are the ones who receive preferential treatment. It's a vicious cycle that for decades has helped maintain the status quo.

While faculty diversity hiring has slowed, Columbia has remained at the forefront of the diversity movement. The school has also doubled down on student diversity, a challenge that Mitchell said is infinitely easier, given fresh opportunities each year to select a new class. The incoming undergraduate class of 2022 was its most diverse ever, with 16 percent Black, 17 percent Latino, 28 percent Asian, and 17 percent first generation.

"As we come into our own, the opposition attacks and demonizes," said Mitchell. "I'm proud of the accomplishments. The challenge now is to sustain an arc of progress. The models are there."[17]

Columbia can sustain its $10 million-a-year investment in diversity for five years, until 2023. The question is, what will happen afterward. "He understands legacy," said Mitchell of Bollinger, who in 2018 entered his seventeenth year at the helm of Columbia. "My intention is to move this toward endowment," which would require an investment of $200 million to endow the entire program. It is an ambitious fundraising goal that will likely compete with other development priorities, but Mitchell is hopeful. "The only security is long-term security. That is the direction."

In the meantime, he said, schools must continually build bridges to steer underrepresented minorities to PhD programs and to STEM. He said schools will continue to be challenged by pipeline issues resulting from the decline of public education. While there are significantly more PhDs among underrepresented minorities, "is it enough to achieve diversity across the nation? Not a chance.... But it's not just the numbers," Mitchell said, alluding to retention and the protests that have gripped college campuses. "It's the climate."

However, Mitchell said he's encouraged by the wave of diversity initiatives now under way at many of Columbia's peer institutions. Since 2015, hundreds of millions of dollars have been pledged to address diversity at other prestigious schools, including a $50 million commitment by Yale, $25 million by Dartmouth, $25 million by Johns Hopkins, $50 million by Cornell, and $165 million by Brown, $100 million of which will be endowed. "We're revisiting things nationally that were supposedly resolved fifty years ago," Mitchell said. "We have short memories. We're reliving and revising."

"It's risky business," added Middleton, noting the backlash diversity initiatives often provoke. "Somebody's got to get through and get over."

Change, Middleton said, requires leadership, resources, and intentionality at the top. "People figured that I could do it alone," he said of the years he spent promoting diversity at the University of Missouri before he became the interim president. "I never had the kind of resources that I needed to really address the problem."

Diversity efforts are not only threatened by the courts, legislatures, and resistance from faculty but can also be undermined by the indifference of leadership, alumni, and patrons.

At Harvard, for the first time in its 380-year history, admitted students for the class of 2021 were slightly more than half non-White. Asian American students comprised 22.2 percent, Blacks 14.6 percent, Hispanics 11.6 percent, and Native Americans or Pacific Islanders 2.5 percent, according to data released by the school. In one year, the non-White population expanded from 47.3 percent to 50.8 percent.

Still, the university was the target of a lawsuit that presents yet another challenge to efforts to expand opportunities for underrepresented students of color while pitting minority groups—each of which has been a target of long-standing discrimination—against one another in disquieting ways. The suit claims the admission of Asian students—who at 22.2 percent are nearly four times their proportion of the US population—is capped by the university. Like Bakke, the students are claiming that Harvard violated Title VI of the Civil Rights Act of 1964 that bars institutions receiving federal funds from discriminating based on race. The situation is not as straightforward as it seems. The lawsuit was filed by Students for Fair Admissions, a group formed by Edward Blum, who for two decades has sought to overturn affirmative action and voting rights laws. Blum was also the force behind *Fisher v. University of Texas*, which did not, as he and other affirmative action opponents hoped, totally vanquish race as a factor in college admissions.

"I think [Blum's] intention is to divide and conquer," said Edna Chun, a higher education consultant and former college administrator.[18] "I don't like what Edward Blum has done in general. His goal is to eliminate affirmative action and he's going to use Asian Americans to get there and he may succeed. We've already made it negligible. I do think there must be ways that allow for consideration groups and their advancement in higher education." She said the Bakke decision favored diversity as an educational value for all, unlike affirmative action, which specifically addresses the needs of the historically—and willfully—disadvantaged. "That means it's there to benefit the education of White students. We're left with a patchwork of means to get to the end."

However, Chun, who has one Asian parent, is troubled by the way in which Harvard appeared to single out and stereotype Asian applicants by routinely giving them low personality scores, one of the qualitative scores used to assess candidates. "Harvard has not been terribly good at the way it's applied their criteria. There are subtle forms of discrimination. Let's enable those who haven't had access to have it. But let's not denigrate another group to do it."

This strategy has precedent. In *Pedigree: How Elite Students Get Elite Jobs*, Lauren Rivera recalls a time in history when elite schools, to curb growing Jewish enrollments, began to focus on the personal character of applicants by assessing their involvement in sports, extracurricular activities, and "perceived 'manliness.'" Merit, she argues "is an ever-evolving, moving target that simultaneously shapes and is shaped by power relations in a given society."[19]

Chun said that despite their reputation as a model minority, Asian Americans face unique challenges. "They have no constituency. No public intellectuals. Many are first generation with no clue what it's like." One only has to recall the Yellow Peril movement against Chinese, which in the 1870s triggered rampant murders, lynching, and property destruction; the Chinese

Exclusion Act of 1882, which prohibited citizenship and immigration of Chinese laborers; or President Roosevelt's Executive Order 9066, which prompted the evacuation and forced internment of tens of thousands of people of Japanese ancestry in US concentration camps during World War II, to consider Asian Americans' harrowing path to citizenship and acceptance. Not until 1952 were citizenship exclusions lifted for Japanese and Koreans. Helen Zia, in *Asian American Dreams*, notes that when African American men secured the right to vote after the Civil War, citizenship was specifically denied to Chinese because they were neither Black nor White. Zia also highlights how some of the seventeen lawsuits brought by Chinese Americans that went to the Supreme Court between 1881 and 1896 laid the groundwork for civil rights legislation filed by African Americans decades later. The 1896 ruling in *Yick Wo v. Hopkins* determined that "race neutral" laws could not be selectively enforced against a racial group.[20] Birthright citizenship was affirmed in 1898 by a case brought by native-born Wong Kim, who was denied reentry into the United States because of his Chinese ancestry.

Moreover, Asian Americans' supposed "model minority" status—due to their median income and SAT scores that have eclipsed those of Whites—overshadows the backlash they've experienced due to their ballyhooed success. Still, the ascendance of Asians in America ignores the widening gap between those at the top—some products of the Immigration Act of 1990 that granted H-1B visas to workers in highly skilled fields like science, technology, engineering, and medicine (STEM)—and those at the unskilled bottom. American income inequality was found to be greatest among Asian Americans, with those at the ninetieth percentile having incomes that are 10.7 times greater than those at the bottom 10 percent. Their 90/10 ratio compared to 9.8 for Blacks and 7.8 percent for Whites and Hispanics.[21]

While the Harvard lawsuit is intended to undermine attempts to consider race in admission decisions, it, perhaps inadvertently, cast a bright light on special privileges that have long advantaged wealthy Whites and conversely disadvantage most minority candidates, Asians included. Court documents filed in the case reveal that applicants with legacy and children of patrons are given special consideration in admissions that disproportionately privileges White applicants, given the longstanding exclusive status of White students at the nearly four-hundred-year-old institution.

Harvard researcher Michael Hurwitz examined 307,643 domestic first-year undergraduate applications to thirty elite schools for fall 2007 and found that primary legacy—an application from a student whose parent(s) attended Harvard—could add 45.1 points to that student's application, meaning that if the school has a 5 percent acceptance rate, the chances of a legacy student's acceptance would increase to 50 percent. It could add 23.3 points for secondary legacy, which includes a sibling or other relative.[22]

Other studies have shown that legacy students are more likely to underperform and pursue less rigorous majors. A *Harvard Crimson* survey of the class of 2021 found that a staggering 30.1 percent of the students was legacy and attended private school.[23] Lauren Rivera's work confirms that highly selective schools such as Harvard reproduce what she calls a "persistence of privilege" for an elite few. Graduates of these schools are given preference as candidates for high-paying jobs that, she argues, are typically correlated with parental income and education. She has found that while 80 percent of children born into families in the top economic quartile will obtain four-year degrees, only 10 percent from the bottom tenth will. And holders of bachelor's degrees make 80 percent more than high school graduates, before factoring in attendance at the most elite schools.[24]

The limited access—both real and perceived—to future privilege has intensified the competition for seats in the most selective schools. The competition has been compounded in recent years by the greater number of applicants applying to multiple schools, the increase in the number of students applying to schools outside their geographical region, and the greater proportion of international students attending US colleges and universities. "It's the whole way it's done and done in secret," said Chun of Harvard's admission practices. "So many anomalies. The only good part is now there's greater transparency."

Although the Harvard lawsuit is, by design, racially divisive, a 2014 survey of registered voters in California found that 69 percent of Asian/Pacific Islander Americans actually favor affirmative action to ensure equity for women and racial minorities in employment and education. "We can't just let the loudest voices in the room represent what our community thinks and needs," said Karthick Ramakrishnan, a UC Riverside professor who coauthored the *National Asian American Survey*.[25] When disaggregated by ethnicity, the greatest support, 73.2 percent, was among Vietnamese and the lowest, 47.1 percent, among Koreans. Nearly 60 percent of Chinese supported affirmative action.

Bollinger worries that even if Harvard wins the legal case, "each challenge chips away at the support for affirmative action and diversity and that's a pity. . . . We are losing because we are not making the case that it's reasonable and good for society. I think you have to have a civil rights consciousness in order to have this really work. You have to believe in a principal of justice. Every institution should speak to this. Instead we've hidden from it. We talk about [diversity] as if it's detached from this history."[26] Bollinger concedes that fear of lawsuits has caused university leaders to shy away from placing diversity in the context of justice.

"I would urge everyone to say it because it needs to be said. I think we've allowed this loss of memory to take hold and the people who oppose it to set the agenda."

But the kind of leaders willing to buck the tide of resistance to diversity from the courts, and the public at large, is apparently in short supply. Few school presidents have appeared willing to go beyond symbolic gestures to substantially expand the pool of underrepresented faculty of color, whose numbers have for decades remained static. If anything, the trend is moving toward a flattened diversity-for-all mantle that embraces diversity of all kinds while ignoring the history and legacy of structural racial disadvantage baked into the educational system.

Whatever success Bollinger has at Columbia will not be enough to move the needle on the number of underrepresented faculty across the broad spectrum of public and private universities unless other presidents are equally willing to find creative ways to navigate over and around the obstacles erected by the courts, legislatures, public sentiment, and the priorities of patrons and alumni. And the most meaningful change must begin long before the college admission process. It must begin, as it did in the 1960s and 1970s, in public schools that have once again largely become separate and unequal.

CHAPTER

6

CORPORATE AMERICA'S JOURNEY TO JUSTICE

*"The Company, its shareholders and all of its employees
will benefit by striving to be a premier 'gold standard'
company on diversity."*
—Statement in settlement agreement in
Ingram v. Coca-Cola Company

In 1995, as a senior vice president and the highest-ranking
African American at the Coca-Cola Company, Carl Ware
oversaw the company's business on the African continent, where
he dined with presidents and was accorded the respect of a visiting dignitary. But at home he couldn't help but notice that
the higher he rose in the company, the Whiter the workforce
became, with Blacks mostly relegated to the bottom rungs of
the corporate ladder. Coca-Cola, an iconic American brand and

among the Fortune 100 most enviable blue chip companies, at the time employed 10,400 people in the United States and 37,400 around the world; it was awash with prosperity.

Ware, a well-connected former Atlanta city council member who had been credited with Coca-Cola's divestment from South Africa during apartheid, began holding meetings where Black employees expressed their sense of alienation and belief that they had been denied upward mobility and a stake in the company's soaring profits. He managed to get company officials to sign off on a study of how the company fared with the hiring, promotion, and retention of its African American employees.

After a month of meetings and assistance from a consulting firm, he issued a report to company CEO Douglas Ivester that was flagged as "HIGHLY RESTRICTIVE—HIGHLY CONFIDENTIAL." The report described a hostile environment for Black employees, who felt undervalued and demeaned. "Instances were mentioned when members had been humiliated, ignored, overlooked, or unacknowledged," the report said. "Even when African Americans were few in number in the organization, an informal network of African Americans was operating to provide sanity checks and a comparison of related experiences with the social realities of the organization. This allowed many of them to retain their psychological health."[1] The report called for the company to address "the lack of tolerance by the organization toward those who are different" and said the company "has no clearly articulated vision of how diversification of the workforce is linked to business success."

For several years, Ware's explosive report would remain private and its findings go largely unheeded. But its rediscovery several years later would help substantiate claims made in a class action discrimination lawsuit that in 2000 resulted in a $192.5 million settlement—the largest for racial discrimination in legal history—with injunctive relief paid to roughly twenty-two hundred Black employees.

The settlement sent shock waves through corporate America, becoming a cautionary tale about the pitfalls of institutional bias. "I wanted to change them," said Cyrus Mehri, the plaintiffs' senior counsel of the company. "It was a social justice movement," he said, one that set Coca-Cola on a quest to being the gold standard for corporate diversity.[2]

The case study is not only instructive for revealing how discrimination metastasizes in an organization but also for showing how, and under what circumstances, a major corporation can change. The settlement, which created a system of outside monitoring of compliance, offered an extraordinary window on a workplace in the throes of change.

The level of scrutiny on Coca-Cola's transformation was, perhaps, unrivalled. Unlike the cloistered worlds of Hollywood, the arts, and academia, which employ a relatively small number of people, corporate America, with its global reach, influences the livelihoods of millions of people on a daily basis. "Many diversity and inclusion officers came about because of the Coca-Cola settlement," said Mehri. "It inspired companies to say, 'We don't want to be the next Texaco or Coca-Cola.' It became the standard that others can follow."

The settlement brought to a head a years-long effort to diversify Coca-Cola's workforce at its corporate headquarters in Atlanta, where in 1973 Maynard Jackson was elected the city's first African American mayor. Atlanta, home to Emory University and Georgia Institute of Technology, along with

Morehouse College, Spelman College, and Clark Atlanta University—among the nation's most prestigious Historically Black Colleges and Universities—boasted an educated African American workforce. While Coca-Cola contributed to a number of high-profile Black causes, its workforce remained bifurcated along racial lines, with Blacks clustered at the bottom and the managers overwhelmingly White and male. This reality was not lost on local and national leaders. In 1981, Rev. Jesse Jackson led a boycott of Coke products that ended with the company vowing to hire more African Americans and award more business to Black bottlers and distributors.

Not much had changed when, in 1988, Linda Ingram joined Coca-Cola to work as an information analyst. For several years, Ingram, who is African American, took pride in her association with the company. But her life there significantly deteriorated in 1996 after she said her White supervisor berated her and allegedly told her, "This is why you people don't get anywhere."[3] Ingram, the only African American in her unit, was stunned and humiliated and reported the incident to human resources. The supervisor was fired, but Ingram's problems only worsened. Many blamed her for the dismissal of the popular supervisor.

Ostracized and depressed, she sought counseling from her pastor and filed for long-term disability leave. She eventually sold her house to keep afloat financially. One day, she came across an article about Bari-Ellen Roberts, the lead plaintiff in *Roberts v. Texaco*, a discrimination lawsuit against Texaco that had in 1996 resulted in a $176 million settlement, then the largest for discrimination in legal history.

Roberts had joined Texaco as a senior financial analyst at the end of 1990 after a successful career on Wall Street. She became the first African American woman in a professional position in Texaco's financial department and attributes her hiring to the scrutiny over Texaco's low numbers of women and minorities following a company audit. The revelation was made in the wake of the lawsuit that Pennzoil Company filed against Texaco over a merger deal that in 1985 resulted in the court ordering Texaco to pay Pennzoil more than $10.5 billion in damages. To protect its assets, Texaco filed for bankruptcy in 1987. "I could cover women and African Americans, forty and over, boom," Roberts said in an interview in 2019 explaining her hiring.[4] "And so we have one; before we had none."

After three years at Texaco, the numbers had not improved, so Roberts and her colleague Sil Chambers met with the vice president of human resources to discuss how Texaco could improve diversity. "We were analysts, so we did the research," Roberts said. "We came to the meeting with the head of HR with our presentation." Roberts outlined initiatives such as recruiting at Historically Black Colleges and Universities. "But before we could get past the salad, the VP of HR looked at us and said, 'Texaco will never do any of these things,' and said, 'You must be Black Panthers.' I was blown away."

A week later, Roberts received an excellent work review, but before her manager could sign off on it, it was downgraded. "I said, 'Why?' And she said, 'You said things to some people here and they're not comfortable with what you said.' The same thing happened to Sil. So we knew what it was."

Slowly, opportunities she once had, such as attendance at conferences, were denied and her supervisor began assigning work with unrealistic deadlines. "The company was trying to play mental games," said Roberts. "I said, 'Sil, we should sue these people. We haven't done anything wrong.' Then we started talking."

"It started out kind of innocently," she said of conversations with colleagues in other divisions about their experiences. "I knew how they were treating me. I didn't know the depths of how they were treating everyone else. I thought it was me."

She said a White female colleague who worked in HR and had previously sued the company confided that there had been African Americans who had worked there for ten years but had never gotten raises or been promoted. The woman also told her that some in management were intent on undermining Roberts.

"When I started seeing the numbers, and hearing the stories, I thought, how can they justify this," Roberts recalled, especially given the company's location some thirty miles from New York City. The question inspired her decision to become a lead plaintiff in the uphill battle against the corporate giant.

Roberts recounted her experience in *Roberts v. Texaco: A True Story of Race and Corporate America*, which she coauthored with the journalist Jack E. White. "Like thousands of other black professionals who moved into the managerial ranks of Fortune 500 companies during the 1980s and 1990s, I had based my life on a myth," Roberts recounted. "I believed it when the men of Texaco assured me that they really meant what they said in their glossy recruiting brochures . . . it was merit, not color, that counted."[5]

Roberts's account resonated with Ingram, who went to meet her at a book signing in Atlanta. After briefly hearing Ingram's story, Roberts slipped Ingram a piece of paper with attorney Cyrus Mehri's name and number. By then Ingram had identified potential coplaintiffs and called Mehri to say she had a case like Texaco's. Mehri went to Atlanta to meet with Ingram and her former colleagues. "The moment I met the clients, I believed in the case," Mehri said.[6]

Flying under the banner of findjustice.com and with a penchant for making news, Mehri fashions himself as an avenger for the underdog. Born to Iranian immigrants in Connecticut, he had been well versed by them in the ways of injustice and the sanctity of democracy. During the Allied occupation of Iran during World War II, Mehri's father, Parviz, and his brother helped US allied troops stationed in Iran by translating Farsi to English. He and his brother were among the first Iranians to pursue an education in the United States when in 1947 the brothers attended Louisiana State University. There, they witnessed firsthand the mistreatment of African Americans. "They weren't treated much better as foreigners," Mehri said.[7]

His father graduated in less than three years and attended Washington University Medical School, from which he earned a degree in ophthalmology. He returned to Iran, where he met and married Mehri's mother, Bahijeh, who had studied at the American University in Beirut. However, it's only after they married that Parviz learned that she had become a target of the secret police of Iran due to her criticism of the government and was restricted from leaving the country. After months of appeals in 1959, Bahijeh was permitted to emigrate to Canada, from where she crossed the bridge at Niagara Falls to arrive in America.

"The values I grew up with was the idealism of the Kennedy era, the Civil Rights Movement," said Mehri, who first visited Washington, DC, as a child during an antiwar protest with his parents. "There was this recognition of how great this country is for democracy and education, life, liberty, and the pursuit of happiness alongside the tragedy of race in America."

After attending what he described as a progressive private school in Connecticut, Mehri went to Hartwick College in upstate New York, and after two years working as a field organizer for the nonprofit consumer advocacy agency Public Citizen attended Cornell Law School. Upon graduating in 1988, he clerked for a year with Judge John Nixon in the US District Court in Nashville. During the 1960s, Nixon had been tapped by Robert Kennedy to work for the Civil Rights Division, where for a time he was charged with protecting Dr. Martin Luther King Jr. during his trips to Selma, Alabama. As a federal judge, Nixon held death row unconstitutional under the Eighth Amendment and overturned a number of death penalty cases. "He was a civil rights icon," Mehri said of Nixon. "I don't know if there was a judge more courageous than he was. He led his life under death threat. Marshals always worried about his safety."

In 1989 Mehri was hired by the Washington, DC, firm Cohen Milstein, where he specialized in antitrust cases. But after doing a pro bono case for Friends of the Earth, he was told about workers at Texaco who were seeking legal counsel. He went to meet with them at a church in White Plains, New York, and was immediately impressed. "These were the Rosa Parks of corporate America," he said. "Nobody's standing up, and they're standing up. They were stellar people with stellar accomplishments. There was a perfection to that feeling in that room." At age thirty-two, Mehri had found his calling.

But when, following the Texaco settlement, Ingram called in early 1998, Mehri had recently declined a partnership at Cohen

Milstein to start his own civil rights practice and didn't yet have an office or staff. While he was intrigued by the case, he believed he'd need a cocounsel to help him take on the corporate behemoth. He approached six major firms that, one by one, turned him down. "They saw it like trying to sue the pope in the Vatican," he said.

But he was buoyed by the arrival of an anonymously sent package that contained a printout of Coca-Cola's entire human resources database. The documents delineated the positions, salaries, and tenure of every employee. The printout substantiated the Black employees' perception of bias, showing that Blacks disproportionately held the lowest-paying jobs and even in senior positions were paid less than their White counterparts. The revelation rivaled an explosive secret tape recording that had been turned over to Mehri in the midst of the Texaco trial. Richard Lundwall, the head of the finance division in Texaco's HR, had offered the tape recording to Roberts after he was laid off.

"There's language on here that's unacceptable in the civilized world," Mehri said Lundwall told him when they met. On the tapes, the senior executives, including Lundwall, are heard discussing the destruction of key evidence that had been subpoenaed in the case. On one of the tapes, Robert Ulrich, then the company treasurer, complains about diversity and is allegedly heard disparaging African American workers as "niggers" and at another point is heard saying, "I'm still having trouble with Hanukkah, and now we have Kwanzaa."[8] Complaining about "this diversity thing," Ulrich said, "You know how all the black jelly beans agree," to which Lundwall replied: "That's funny. All the black jelly beans seem to be glued to the bottom of the bag."[9] The tapes, a portion of which was broadcast on ABC's *Nightline* during an interview with Texaco CEO Peter Bijur, was the smoking gun that would bring the case that had dragged on for more than two years to a swift conclusion.[10]

But while that settlement prompted diversity reforms at Texaco, they were apparently not enough to spark substantive change at Coca-Cola. "Everyone thought lightning would strike somewhere else," Mehri said. The court gave Mehri 120 days between filing and serving the papers to Coca-Cola to decide whether to take on the company alone. By the 119th day, he still remained the sole counsel. "I had to make a decision whether I was willing to bet my entire well-being on this case without a cocounsel."

On April 22, 1999, Mehri, without a cocounsel, filed the lawsuit in the US District Court in Atlanta, accusing the company of systematic racial discrimination. The first story appeared in the *New York Times* on April 23, 1999, under the headline "Blacks, Citing Bias at Work, Sue Coca-Cola." The lawsuit claimed that Blacks consistently received lower pay, fewer promotions, and unsatisfactory performance evaluations. While the median salary for Blacks was $36,596, it was $65,531—nearly 100 percent more—for Whites.

The lawsuit cited an instance where a Black woman made less than those who reported to her. African Americans held 15.7 percent of the jobs but comprised 37 percent of the support staff. Only 1.5 percent were in senior management. Ware remained the only African American senior vice president out of thirteen in the company. The lawsuit said a glass wall kept Blacks from securing positions in marketing and finance.

George Eddings Jr., one of the four named plaintiffs, had already left the company by the time the lawsuit was filed.

Eddings, with an MBA from the University of Chicago, had worked at Amaco Corporation for three years before joining Coca-Cola in 1992 as a field research manager. "I was loving my life in Houston," said Eddings, who worked for Minute Maid, a division of Coca-Cola.[11] But he became disenchanted when he went to his supervisor seeking a promotion and raise in response to an outside offer. Eddings reported that his supervisor said he could not do anything and that the matter was out of his hands. Eddings later learned that a White woman in a position similar to his was being wooed for the very position he sought but had turned it down. Shortly after, he was recruited to Campbell Soup Company, where he began working in 1997. He was at Campbell Soup when news of the pending lawsuit reached him.

"I said 'sign me up,'" he recalls, still rankled two decades later by his manager's snub. "Folks were advising me it could limit future employment opportunities," Eddings said. "That's something I really had to weigh. But this was the right thing to do for the right reason. I wanted to have my voice heard."

The story made headlines across the country and around the world, including in every leading newspaper in the country, including the *Wall Street Journal*, *USA Today*, and the *Atlanta Constitution*. Ivester, who according to the complaint had said it would take fifteen to twenty years before African Americans were well represented among senior management, dismissed the claims as baseless and vowed to fight. He penned a company-wide email in which he contended, "Our company has always endeavored to treat our customers, our consumers, our bottlers and, perhaps most importantly, our employees with fairness, respect, and dignity." Given its track record, he said, the lawsuit "is so troubling to me."[12]

A month later, Ivester did what many institutions do when they fall under a public cloud of discrimination: he announced the formation of a Diversity Council that would be cochaired by Ware and Jack Stahl, the senior vice president for North America, and report to him. Of course, he had not taken such action when he received Ware's report several years earlier, but that report had remained shrouded in secrecy. He now told employees that the advisory council would "assure that we are able to achieve our different, better and special standard and to maximize the benefits of diversity in our work force." He said he would "personally increase my own efforts to open the lines of communication with all constituencies."[13] Ivester said he would hold regular meetings with the council that would be led by Ware.

As Coca-Cola, with its phalanx of lawyers, prepared its defense, Mehri braced himself for a bloody, David v. Goliath–style battle. With his three-person firm up against a bottomless reservoir of capital and prestige, and some of the nation's most venerable law firms—including Paul Hastings, Janofsky & Walker, and King and Spalding—Mehri took out a seven-figure loan to be able to stay in the ring.

But by November 1999, some seven months after the lawsuit was filed, Coca-Cola's wall of invincibility began to crumble. That's when Ware—at age fifty-six and still the sole African American senior vice president and cochair of the Diversity Council—announced his early retirement. His public statement, carefully calibrated and likely run through Coca-Cola's corporate public relations office, read, in part, "Personally, I want to be able to spend more time with my wife, my son, and my grandchildren."[14]

But it soon came to light that in the restructuring at Coca-Cola, Ware—the only African American senior vice president in the company's 113-year history—was essentially demoted when he was told he would no longer report to the chairman and CEO. Ware, the one person Coca-Cola could hope would offset discrimination allegations, was no longer a convenient excuse. The company's cavalier handling of Ware indicated its disinterest in the issues the plaintiffs had raised. Within days of press accounts of Ware's poorly timed demotion, Warren Buffett and Herbert Allen Jr., the billionaire members of Coca-Cola's board of directors, flew to Chicago to meet with Ivester. The meeting that December culminated in the fifty-two-year-old CEO unexpectedly announcing his retirement. "You could argue that the stupid decision with Carl Ware ended Ivester's stewardship at Coca-Cola," Mehri said. It also came on the heels of a controversy over the company's slow response to tainted cans of Coke in Belgium.

The board announced that Ivester's successor would be Douglas N. Daft, a Coca-Cola executive from Australia who had been with the company for thirty years.

Then that same month, Ware's private 1995 memo came to light. The plaintiff's lawsuit was amended to note that company officials had long known about African Americans' claims of institutional bias.

While Daft was not officially installed until April, he took immediate control. In January 2000, he announced an organizational alignment that would cut six thousand jobs worldwide and some twenty-five hundred in Atlanta, amounting to nearly half of its workforce, a shake-up that, intentionally or not, eclipsed the plaintiffs' claims of bias.

The Black employees targeted for dismissal were told that in order to receive a severance package they must waive their right to join the pending lawsuit. By then, Mehri had found a cocounsel—Bondurant, Mixson & Elmore LLP, which had previously sued Coca-Cola and was well connected in Atlanta. Together, they filed a motion saying the waiver would impose a burden on African American employees. A federal judge ordered Coca-Cola to clarify that the employees could participate as witnesses or sources of evidence and still receive enhanced benefits. However, signing the waiver would mean they could not be part of the class.

In obvious damage-control mode, Daft convinced Ware to rescind his resignation to serve as executive vice president overseeing a newly created global public affairs division. He would again report directly to the CEO and be in charge of global communications, government relations, and corporate external affairs. The recognizable strategy of placing African Americans in prominent positions to deflect from racial controversy did not dissuade Coca-Cola—or many companies thereafter—from employing it. As noted earlier, in 2019 the fashion company Prada followed the same course to rebound from scandal. While Ware had previously been regarded as dispensable, he would now resume his responsibilities as cochair of the diversity council and be an advisor to his successor in Africa. Apparently, Ware no longer wished to spend more time with his family, as he had claimed in his retirement statement.

Mehri was quick to call Coca-Cola out on the blatant tokenism. "I think the real question for Daft is not making one promotion, but whether he will have the guts and vision to put an end to the barriers thwarting the careers of African Americans throughout the company," Mehri said at the time.[15]

Daft also announced the creation of a $1 billion fund to award contracts to and invest in businesses owned by Blacks and by women. The amount doubled the company's commitment to diversity programs.

"This is a business strategy," said Ware after the sudden announcement. "It's not something that's tacked on because it's a nice thing to do, although it is the right thing to do."[16] The company also announced it would invest $1 billion in Africa over the next three years to fund new bottling and canning plants, marketing, and the acquisition of new brands.

But none of Coca-Cola's tactics would stop the mounting fury of the workers, who began to organize protests, including a planned showdown in Wilmington, Delaware, at what would be Daft's first board meeting as the CEO, in April. Rev. Jesse Jackson and leaders of the Southern Christian Leadership Conference (SCLC) publicly urged the company to settle the lawsuit before the workers' planned "Bus Ride for Justice." "This is a strategy that the employees have come up with and that we feel compelled to support," said Martin Luther King III, then president of the SCLC.[17] Former and current Black employees arrived in Wilmington by bus wearing red hats emblazoned with "Justice Ride." Larry Jones, a laid-off human resources manager who organized the protest, proposed a boycott. "In 114 years, you only found one of us qualified?" Jones, alluding to Ware, said before some seven hundred investors at the shareholders meeting. "How long do we wait?"[18]

Rev. Jesse Jackson, a shareholder in Coca-Cola, urged the board to settle the lawsuit and expressed disappointment in the board's lack of commitment to diversity, as demonstrated not only by the allegations of its Black workers but also by the composition of the board. He noted that in twenty years there had been only one African American on the board and no Hispanics, although Hispanics comprised, at the time, 27 percent of Coke consumers. He also criticized the company for not replacing Ware with an African.

"Coke is the largest employer in Africa," Jackson said. "Coke has infrastructure, sugar planters, water plants, and yet no African succeeded Carl Ware." Jackson urged the company to "choose negotiation over confrontation. Choose resolution over boycott. Change the culture."[19] Daft, in response, insisted that the company was the most diverse in the world. "We could always do better. No one is perfect. We will be the company that leads the world into a diverse business structure in the 21st century."[20] The rhetoric did little good. Besieged by bad publicity, Coca-Cola, which had initially vowed it would not settle the lawsuit, reached a tentative settlement on June 7, 2000, that was approved by the US District Court for the Northern District of Georgia. By November, the company agreed to a $192.5 million settlement that included $113 million in cash payouts to salaried Black employees in the United States who worked for the company between April 22, 1995, and June 14, 2000. The amount paid out averaged $40,000 per employee, while the four named plaintiffs would each receive up to $300,000. Another $43.5 million was allocated to adjust salaries, and $36 million for oversight of the company's employment practices. In addition, the company paid $20 million in attorneys' fees to a total of three law firms representing the class and pledged to contribute $50 million to its foundation for community initiatives.

"The Coca-Cola Company commits to excel among Fortune 500 Companies in promoting and fostering equal opportunity in compensation, promotion, and career advancement for all employees in all levels and areas of the business, regardless of race, color, gender, religion, age, national origin, or disability, and to promote and foster an environment of inclusion, respect and freedom from retaliation," read the agreement.[21]

The company reasserted the standard line about diversity being a "fundamental and indispensable" company value, but it went further by saying it would strive to become the corporate gold standard.

"It felt huge and groundbreaking," recalled Eddings upon reflection twenty years later. But "a multibillion-dollar corporation wrote that off in the fourth quarter."[22] Indeed, the company had, the previous year, reported $20 billion in sales and said it would charge the payout to its fourth quarter. In retrospect, Eddings was not convinced that the amount was enough to incentivize systemic change.

Perhaps it alone would not. However, a cornerstone of the settlement was the formation of a seven-member task force to serve as watchdogs to ensure that the company complied with the agreement. The same measure was taken following the Texaco settlement. The task force was chaired by Alexis Herman, an appointee of President Bill Clinton who in 1997 had become the first African American to serve as US secretary of labor. In April 2001, Coca-Cola hired another former Clinton appointee, Deval Patrick, to serve as its general counsel. Patrick had served as US assistant attorney general for the Civil Rights Division. In 1997, he was appointed by the federal district court to chair the task force overseeing the $176 million Texaco discrimination settlement. A year later he became general counsel at Texaco, where he continued to help lead the company's reform efforts.

In 2006, Patrick would be elected governor of Massachusetts and serve from 2007 to 2015.

The settlement called for the company to address some of the systemic and cultural issues that the lawsuit had highlighted. Among Coca-Cola's mandates was the development of a system that would result in fair compensation, promotion, and evaluation, and a commitment to setting "measurable and lawful business goals" to achieve that aim.[23] Coca-Cola appointed an ombudsman to investigate complaints and submit annual reports to Daft and periodic reports to the task force. The settlement also required Coca-Cola's board of directors to monitor progress by reviewing and amending, as needed, policies on salaries, promotions, merit pay, bonuses and stock options, and evaluations; compiling employment data; and improving workplace conditions, and said new board members should also reflect a commitment to diversity.

Under the watchful eyes of the task force, the company, by all appearances, began to change.

The first task report, issued in July 2002, demonstrated the task force's rigor and resolve. It commended Coca-Cola's efforts toward revamping its system for determining salaries, promotions, and raises to ensure fairness. They had devised a central pay scale for roles aligned with the market and routed prospective candidates' offers to the corporate legal department in advance. The company had also designed an external recruitment program to build a diverse candidate pipeline.

However, it noted that the company had not considered diversity and inclusion when appointing new board members at its spring shareholder's meeting. The company, it said, "must not only say it is committed to diversity, but must demonstrate that commitment through its actions."[24]

The task force chided the company for not consulting it or considering diversity before nominating two board members. The action, it said, "suggested a lack of sensitivity to declared diversity goals."

The report said Daft had since met with the task force and assured members they would be consulted in the selection of future board members. The report also took note of a climate survey that showed "a distinct gap" between White and racial and ethnic minorities over perceptions of fairness related to equal opportunity. The survey showed that African Americans were less inclined than White employees to believe the company was fair in regard to promotions and career development.

Over the next four years, the climate and composition of Coca-Cola's workplace began to change, first gradually, as the task force nudged and sometimes dragged the company into compliance with the court agreement. A detailed, system-wide assessment involving data collection and review measured the actual numbers of people hired, promoted, and recruited along racial and gender lines, creating transparency and accountability.

Steve Bucherati had been at the company working in human resources for global marketing when, following the settlement, he was asked to oversee company diversity efforts. "We want you to fix it," he said he was told. "I spent the next fourteen years fixing it," said Bucherati, who for more than a decade served as the company's global chief diversity officer.[25] Over lunch with Mehri, he gained insight into ways to gauge workplace fairness along racial and gender lines. "We will measure, quantitatively, everything that touches an employee to ensure that everything we're doing is right and fair," Bucherati said. He gathered data across the company. "I wanted to do triage, not forensics," he said, explaining that looking at the data before performance ratings, job offers, stock option grants, and promotions were finalized allowed the company to address issues in real time, before inequality became systemic. "We would do regression modeling on proposed bonuses. This would allow us to see disparities. Who's being negatively impacted?"

Coca-Cola measured progress toward diversity in nine key areas: performance management, staffing, compensation, diversity education, equal employment opportunity, problem resolution, career development, succession planning, and mentoring.

By the second task force report, the company had appointed two people of color to the board. While the lawsuit was filed by African Americans, it's worth noting that neither of the two board members, a man and a woman, were Black. Both were Hispanic. The task force said the company had made progress in the promotion of minorities and women in executive, managerial, and professional jobs during the last six months of 2002. However, it said, "disparities developed between African American and white employees receiving promotions . . . in the first six months of 2003, particularly in the promotion rates of African American and white males for executive and managerial jobs."[26]

The task force noted that it was especially "troubled" by a trend of promotions in the top-level grades, "reflecting an absence of diversity." It noted that the company had not changed its interview process nor developed diverse candidate slates, reminding the company that the mobility of African Americans was at the heart of the lawsuit and the settlement agreement.

The task force urged Coca-Cola to affirm its commitment to diversity as a critical component of its strategy by linking diversity to its business goals and to executive compensation "as required by the Agreement." It said that the company must demonstrate progress by the next review cycle.

Between that report and the next one in 2004, Coca-Cola appointed E. Neville Isdell as its new chairman and CEO. Isdell, along with the new senior vice president of human resources, Cynthia McCague, requested that the term of the task force be extended a year to help guide the company's diversity plan. Under the settlement agreement, the term of the task force would otherwise expire December 2005. On November 24, 2004, Judge Richard Story issued an order formalizing the extension to December 2006.

Under Isdell, the company made its greatest leap toward its goal of becoming a "gold standard." Isdell, a native of Ireland who had moved to Zambia at age ten, had spent the formative years of his life in southern Africa. He received his undergraduate education at the University of Cape Town and joined the Coca-Cola Company in 1966. By 1972, he was the general manager of Coca-Cola Bottling of Johannesburg, South Africa. He continued to move up the ladder, becoming the manager of Coca-Cola's Central European Division in 1985, and four years later became a group president for Northeast Europe, the Middle East, and Africa.

Bucherati recalls Isdell's first day in his new role, which coincided with the first day of a three-day task force meeting. "Neville walked into the room and said, 'I am here with you. I want to learn and make sure Coca-Cola moves in the right direction.' From day one, he led from the front."[27]

The following year, the task force reported "substantial improvement" in diversity in new hires in the upper grades of the company. "More than 51% of new hires at grade 14 and above were minorities, with African Americans accounting for 35.9% of the new hires," the report said.[28] Among its senior leadership, the company had elected and appointed new officers: while in 2000, 16 percent of these officers were female, and 8 percent were minority; in 2005, the numbers were 27 percent and 21 percent, respectively.

"That is a 68% increase in women and a 161% increase minority membership within the officer ranks in a five-year time span," the report said.[29]

The company also had made progress in diversifying its pipeline of talent to fill midlevel positions. In one year, between 2004 and 2005, the increase in minorities in grades 10 to 13 increased by 3 percent, to nearly 26 percent. That represented a 21 percent increase since 2002.

Still, the report found that African American and Asian American employees more negatively assessed the fairness of the promotion process than Whites, Hispanics, or women.

"The Company is appropriately attempting to move from a culture of compliance with the Settlement Agreement, through a process of commitment to the principles and spirit of the Settlement Agreement and ultimately to an inclusive, collaborative workplace culture in which diversity efforts and processes are institutionalized," the task force report said.

Among the remaining tasks of concern were the continued monitoring of training, particularly in middle management; the hiring process; and the monitoring of performance ratings. "Of particular concern to the Task Force is ensuring that the staffing and selection process is fair and determining whether there have been missed opportunities for women and minorities, particularly African American candidates."

The task force found that the selection rate patterns for African Americans were lower than expected when compared to the interview pools. "The Company should promptly determine possible causes of the observed differences in these selection rates."

Strict oversight and monitoring of performance, management, and staffing was still necessary to prevent backsliding "particularly to the detriment of African Americans," the task force maintained. It requested the company to report on its progress on its systems of accountability and fairness by March 2006.

The lack of a "cogent and sustained" diversity strategy remained a concern, but the task force applauded Coca-Cola's efforts to integrate diversity into its business objectives in its "Manifesto for Growth." However, it said it needed to go further. The report also said the company had shown progress in the implementation of its human resources accountability system but encouraged vigilance in order to sustain it and change the company culture.

The task force filed its final report on December 2006 and reported "major strides" by the company, noting that the company had designed a strategy to make diversity an integral part of its human resources, marketing, philanthropy, and supplier strategies.[30]

Coca-Cola had also activated its Diversity Advisory Councils, comprised of senior company leaders, and employee forums to engage employees on its mission. The council would develop strategies and initiatives and monitor progress and the company's diversity metrics to ensure ongoing compliance with stated goals.

The task force lauded the company for the system it created to arrive at performance, management, staffing, and compensation decisions and said human resources had become an indispensable part of the leadership team, enabling the company to monitor progress and make needed corrections. It advised the company to continue monitoring performance evaluation, staffing, and compensation systems through regular audits. The task force also advocated continued training to integrate diversity in all human resource practices and the conducting of annual climate surveys.

Coca-Cola had managed to create a model that not only transformed its workplace but that could also be replicated by other institutions. While many managers may believe they are capable of making decisions that are free of race and gender bias, the objective metrics implemented by Coca-Cola created transparency and allowed senior management to monitor practices system-wide. The company's progress toward diversity would require vigilant monitoring to avoid relapsing.

The task force concluded that Coca-Cola had made "substantial progress" since the settlement agreement and while there was room for improvement, senior management had demonstrated its commitment to diversity and fairness and showed that companies—even large legacy institutions like Coca-Cola—could change.

"The company's goal," it said, "must be to build on the successes and constantly strive to be the 'gold standard' company for inclusion and fairness."

Isdell had committed to continuing the journey without relying on an outside watchdog. In the midst of year five of the task force's work, Bucherati said Isdell walked into a meeting unannounced and assured members of his commitment to their efforts. "I'm here to commit to you that we will sustain all of your work for years beyond your existence," Bucherati recalled Isdell saying. He said at the end of the process Isdell, Judge Story, Mehri, and the task force members celebrated their work after a meeting in federal court. "Everybody came into this with the right mindset."[31]

"It took a village of people to make this successful, people of all backgrounds lending themselves to strategies, initiatives, minutia. It took so many talented people," Bucherati continued. He credits Mehri and the task force, which, he said, "approached us the right way. In the years that followed, we became best in class."

In 2005 Isdell, speaking before the Executive Leadership Council, a group that aims to advance the progress of African American executives, called the episode in the company's history "an embarrassment." "If our performance is going to continue to improve, it's imperative that we leverage our global diversity more effectively," he told the group. "We must ensure that we lead in a multicultural world."[32] As an expression of his commitment, he announced a $1 million donation to the group.

In 2006, Coca-Cola made the *Black Enterprise* magazine list of the 40 Best Companies for Diversity. The same year, it was listed as number three on the top fifty list of *Diversity, Inc.* magazine, and the company was recognized by the US Hispanic Chamber of Commerce.

In 2008, upon his retirement as CEO, Isdell was succeeded by Muhtar Kent, who had been Isdell's second in command. The momentum toward diversity continued under Kent, the New York–born son of a Turkish diplomat, who had been raised in Turkey, Iran, Thailand, and India.

In 2012, Kent championed the creation of a Multicultural Leadership Council that created Multicultural EDGE, a week-long leadership development program for emerging leaders. The group expanded its efforts by launching Diversity 50, a year-long leadership development program to shore up the leadership pipeline. Reflecting Kent's focus on women empowerment, it launched "#5by20," an initiative aimed at supporting the economic empowerment of five million women entrepreneurs by 2020. Under Kent, the number of women on Coca-Cola's fifteen-member board increased from two to four and included two African American women and one Hispanic woman. In 2016, Kent topped the inaugural UPstanding Executive Power List for his championship of diverse and inclusive workplaces. The list was published by Audeliss, a global executive search firm.

The improvements continued, if gradually. Between 2011 and 2016, the percentage of racial and ethnic minorities working in the Atlanta headquarters expanded from 40 percent to 43 percent. At the end of 2017 the company said its US workforce composition was 32.3 percent "multicultural." In an interview in February 2019, Ann Moore, the company's communications director, said that 177—or 24.3 percent—of the company's 727-member leadership team was Black, Asian, and Hispanic. (A small percentage, 1.7 percent was "Other.") Of the 177, only Asians, at 6.5 percent, had achieved proportional representation.

Both Hispanics (9.8 percent) and Blacks (6.7 percent) remained disproportionally underrepresented.

But with forty-nine African Americans at the level of vice president and above, the company had come a long way from 2002 when Ware was the only Black senior executive and people of color were just 8 percent of senior management. Among the African American executives were Robert Long, the chief innovations officer; Kathy N. Waller, the executive vice president and chief financial officer who had joined the company in 1987 as a senior accountant; and Craig Williams, the senior vice president and president of the McDonald's division. In 2018, Williams left to become president of Nike's Jordan Brand. Helen Smith Price, the president of Coca-Cola's Foundation, was also African American.

Moore acknowledged that African Americans in senior management were still trailing other groups. "It's a journey. We certainly want to get better but we've come a long, long way from where we were. We're not resting on our laurels."[33]

7

ROONEY'S RULE

"The football field is level. But the same playing field is not level for African American coaches."
—Report, *Black Coaches in the National Football League: Superior Performance, Inferior Opportunities*

Cyrus Mehri was reading the newspaper sports section, as he did each morning, when he learned that Tony Dungy, coach of the NFL's Tampa Bay Buccaneers, had been fired. The news was especially jarring on the 2002 Martin Luther King Day holiday and a little more than a week after the firing of Minnesota Vikings coach Dennis Green. Green and Dungy were among the five African American NFL head coaches in the league's entire eighty-year history.

Like Dungy, Green was a seasoned coach with a winning record. During the 1990s, Green had taken the Vikings to the playoffs in eight of ten seasons and in 1998 was 15-1.

During his ten years as head coach, he had won 63 percent of his games, competed for four division titles, and twice advanced to the NFC Championship.

Dungy became an assistant coach for the Pittsburgh Steelers in 1981 when the league had no head coaches of color. In 1996, he became head coach of the Buccaneers, a team that had not qualified for a playoff in fourteen years. In his second year, the team made it to the playoffs and had ten wins and six losses. Two years later, the team won their division. With Dungy's firing, the number of African American coaches during the 2002 NFL season dropped to one.

"Both were unjust firings," Mehri recalled years later.[1] "I had a hypothesis that Black coaches win more games, go to playoffs more often. I thought, we can do something about this." Mehri assigned an intern to create a database with the win and loss records of NFL coaches, designated by race, over the previous fifteen years. He turned over those numbers to Janice Madden, a labor economist at the University of Pennsylvania, who found statistically significant disparities in hiring and retention along racial lines that suggested discrimination. She found that Black coaches, on average, won 1.1 more games per season and led their teams to the playoffs 67 percent of the time, compared to 39 percent for White coaches.

The findings, along with the historical analysis of team hiring records, were detailed in *Black Coaches in the National Football League: Superior Performance, Inferior Opportunities*, a report Mehri coauthored with attorney Johnnie Cochran Jr., the trial lawyer who had already achieved international fame for his successful defense of former NFL player O. J. Simpson in the murder trial of his wife, Nicole.

With the report's publication, Mehri and Cochran fixed a spotlight on inequities in professional sports—a sphere often perceived as operating on a level playing field irrespective of race. They highlighted how racial diversity—a hallmark of most professional sports, given the large number of players of color—is nearly excluded at the top. They also contended that the handful of Black coaches are held to a higher standard. The critique, while leveled at the NFL, had ramifications across professional sports in the United States and abroad.

"Football is America's game," began the report. "Each week people of all backgrounds discuss, debate, celebrate and agonize—together—over the fortunes and disappointments of their teams."[2] They said they prepared the report because they too loved the sport and believed it should reflect the nation's diversity and values.

But they concluded that it did not. Among their findings was that year after year qualified Blacks were passed over for coaching opportunities, while the few who were hired were more likely to inherit underachieving teams that still outperformed their White peers by winning more games and going more often to the Super Bowl. Compounding the disparity was that nearly 70 percent of NFL players were African American.

"Statistical analysis thus demonstrates that by virtually every objective criteria, black head coaches in the NFL have outperformed their white counterparts," the report maintained. "The cruel counterpart to the superior performance of black coaches in the NFL is inferior hiring opportunities."[3]

The report said that while Black coaches are the last hired, NFL owners were more faithful to losing White coaches than they were to winning Black ones. Moreover, none of the league's thirty-two teams were owned by non-Whites, and just one had a non-White general manager. The report highlighted glaring examples of candidates of color being overlooked for coaching opportunities.

The report noted that in 2000 each of the nine openings were filled by Whites with little or no head coaching experience or losing records. Meanwhile, Sherman Lewis, with four Super Bowl rings and fourteen years of experience, was not interviewed, nor was Emmitt Thomas, a Hall of Fame former defensive coordinator and a highly regarded defensive assistant for twenty-one years. Art Shell, who in 1989 had become head coach of the Los Angeles Raiders—the first Black coach in the NFL since the 1920s—was overlooked as well. Marvin Lewis, who as defensive coordinator helped the Baltimore Ravens get to and win the Super Bowl in 2000, was interviewed but was told he was not a serious candidate. "He never received a tour of the team's facilities, nor was he invited to meet with the team's real decision-makers," according to the report.

In 2001, of the six head coaches hired, one was African American, and of seven coaches hired in 2002, only one, Tony Dungy, was African American. His hiring, however, did not increase the overall number of minority coaches, because eight days after being fired as head coach of the Tampa Bay Buccaneers, Dungy was hired by the Indianapolis Colts. That year, 67 percent of NFL players were Black, but the number of African American head coaches had dropped from three to two, comprising only 6 percent of the head coaching ranks.

"Year after year, franchises pass up the opportunity to interview qualified African American coaching candidates, dispelling the myth that the NFL is a meritocracy," the report said.

In September, a little more than eight months after Dungy's firing, Mehri and Cochran held a press conference in Baltimore to release their report. Later that night, the Baltimore Ravens would face the Denver Broncos at home. While only a handful of reporters attended the news conference, the story "took off like wildfire," recalled Mehri. However, the nuance of the report may have been lost in Cochran's headline-grabbing threat to sue unless the NFL took action. "We can litigate this," Cochran told reporters. "We can bring a lawsuit. I think the NFL is reasonable. They understand that this can end up in the courts, and they'd rather not see that happen. But let's see if we can have a dialogue."[4]

The report by the two prominent civil rights lawyers was bound to command the league's attention. However, years later, Jeff Pash, the league's executive vice president and general counsel, said he thought the report was "somewhat sensationalized" and that threats of a legal case lacked merit. "The NFL, the commissioner's office doesn't hire coaches. We don't decide who gets interviewed, who gets hired. That's 100 percent the purview of the teams." But he added, "that doesn't mean it was devoid of substance. You can't deny the statistics; how many coaches that were hired, how many openings there had been."[5]

The NFL, like other major American institutions, was conscious of its public image. Beyond Mehri and Cochran's command of the courtroom was their knack for showmanship and garnering press. Cochran was by then legendary for his role in the Simpson trial. Cochran memorably told the jurors, "If it doesn't fit, you must acquit," after Simpson appeared to struggle pulling on a glove believed to have been left at the scene by the killer. Meanwhile, Mehri had successfully waged a number of high-profile discrimination lawsuits against powerful companies, including Texaco and Coca-Cola.

Pash invited the lawyers to meet at the NFL's New York City Park Avenue office the week after the press conference. "Rather than empty threats of litigation, let's do something constructive," he said.[6] Cochran was unavailable but days later Mehri met with Pash, Harold Henderson, the league's then executive vice president for labor relations, and Tom Williamson, a well-known Washington litigator who was a partner at the prestigious Covington & Burling who provided outside counsel to the league. Mehri not only knew Williamson by reputation but also respected the role he had played as chair of Texaco's Task Force on Equality and Fairness formed in the aftermath of the discrimination settlement to provide oversight on the company's compliance.

Pash outlined some of the league's past diversity efforts, including its NFL Minority Fellowship Program and a number of coaching symposia and discussions it had held with African American coaches over the years. "If anyone looked at what we tried to do, it would support a conclusion that the league office was trying to promote equal opportunity and diversity, and not doing anything to retard it," Pash said.[7]

Mehri had already been apprised of those initiatives by John Wooten, a former NFL player who had worked in numerous front office jobs and had long advocated for greater opportunities for African American coaches. Wooten had reached out to offer his assistance to Mehri following the release of the report. While Mehri believed Pash was sincere, he maintained that past NFL efforts had clearly not resulted in equal opportunity for African Americans. Other tactics, he argued, were needed.

He and Cochran proposed an NFL rule mandating teams to include at least one candidate of color in the pool of applicants interviewed for head coaching jobs. It also proposed that teams that violated the rule forfeit a first-round draft pick.

As an indication of the seriousness with which the report was received, then-NFL commissioner Paul Tagliabue disseminated copies to each team and held weekly meetings to discuss it. Pittsburgh Steelers president Dan Rooney proposed the creation of a diversity committee of team owners, which Tagliabue acted on, appointing Rooney as its chair. The other members were Arthur Blank of the Atlanta Falcons, Pat Bowlen of the Denver Broncos, Stan Kroenke of the St. Louis Rams, and Jeffrey Lurie of the Philadelphia Eagles. A second committee of club executives was formed with members including Ozzie Newsome, the Baltimore Ravens' senior vice president of football operations; and Ray Anderson, who before working for the Atlanta Falcons represented many of the NFL's aspiring African American coaches; as well as Tony Dungy and Herman Edwards, at the time the league's only African American head coaches.

As the owners explored ways to address the problems raised in the report, Gene Upshaw, the executive director of the NFL Players' Association, voiced his vehement objection to a proposal to penalize teams that did not interview minority head coaches for front office jobs. "It's ridiculous," he said. "You can't say, 'If you do this you'll get some picks," and, 'If you don't do this, you'll lose picks.' You'll end up with sham interviews and sham [candidates] lists." He also expressed resentment over Cochran's role in the discussions. "Someone else talking about it is fine."[8]

A few days later, Rooney also dismissed the draft pick penalty as "totally outlandish."[9] "This is a very competitive business, and teams will not accept that." He added that the diversity committee hoped to have a plan in place before the next head coach hiring cycle. "We're going to talk with every team in the league to see what input they can have and what their own plans are. We're not just talking about head coaches. We're talking about the front offices and assistant coaches. We want to be all-inclusive."[10]

Pash said the brilliance of Rooney was that he early on realized that the responsibility for diversity lay with the owners, not with the league. Pash said he told Tagliabue, "You can help us but ultimately the responsibility belongs to teams and teams owners."[11]

By late November, less than two months after the report's release, a team made NFL history. The Baltimore Ravens announced that Hall of Famer and Super Bowl champion Ozzie Newsome—who was serving on the league's diversity committee—would become the team's general manager, the first African American in the NFL to serve in that position. Team owner Art Modell praised Newsome as the architect of the Super Bowl team two years before and said, "He's the mastermind behind the transition we're undergoing right now."[12]

Then in December 2002, the NFL owners unanimously agreed to adopt the rule Cochran and Mehri had proposed requiring teams to include at least one candidate of color in every head coach search or face a possible fine. Explaining how it became known as the "Rooney Rule," Mehri said, "There was no one more respected in sports—and I wanted them to own it."[13] In 2009, the rule was expanded to include general managers, and in 2016 it was extended to female league office job candidates. The rule still does not require teams to interview women for coaching positions.

Since the rule was adopted, the percentage of Black and other coaches of color rose from 6 percent—or two coaches—to a high of 25 percent—or eight coaches—during a single season. And four years after its adoption, in 2007, Dungy—an impetus of the movement and head coach of the Colts—became the first African American head coach to lead a team to a Super Bowl win. The feat was especially historic given that the opposing team, the Chicago Bears, was coached by Lovie Smith, another African American. In 2013, Dungy was ranked by ESPN among the NFL's twenty greatest coaches of all time.

The Rooney Rule's nominal success—and without cost to NFL teams—made it appealing to other companies. In recent years, Amazon, Facebook, and Uber, all of which faced mounting criticism for their negligible diversity, were among the major companies to announce adoption of the rule. Adopting the rule, however, won't necessarily result in change. For example, in 2018, Amazon, which had no people of color on its ten-member board, said its adoption of the rule would merely formalize its practice of interviewing at least one woman and one person of color for each executive opening. It was unclear how the rule would be enforced. Unlike the NFL, which is in the public spotlight and provides oversight and enforcement of the rule, Amazon would apparently operate on an honor system.

In 2017, Uber released its first diversity report, which showed that there were no Blacks or Hispanics in leadership positions. "This clearly has to change—a diversity of backgrounds and experience is important at every level," the report said.[14] A year later, it had not changed. The workforce was 48.6 percent White, 32.3 percent Asian, 8.1 percent Black, 6.1 percent Hispanic, and 4.3 percent multiracial. The percentage of Blacks had slightly dipped, while Blacks and Latinos in tech positions were 2.6 percent and 3 percent, respectively. Uber pledged $3 million to work with organizations to increase the number of underrepresented groups in tech.

The rule has been applied far beyond the NFL to England's National Football League for manager positions and has been proposed to address the diversity problem in Hollywood and academia.

Mehri acknowledged that the Rooney Rule only works if there's oversight. "They're going through the motions," Mehri said of some of the companies that have adopted it. "Who's actually enforcing it? If someone doesn't own carrying it out, it doesn't happen. You need accountability."[15]

In March 2003, some six months after Mehri and Cochran released their report, Mehri announced the creation of the Fritz Pollard Alliance, named for the Hall of Fame player and the league's first African American coach, to promote equal opportunity in the league. The group, consisting of minority coaches, game day officials, scouts, and front office personnel, continues to serve as a watchdog of the league. Mehri is the group's pro bono cocounsel. "When I started the Rooney Rule movement with Johnnie Cochran, reporters said, 'Cyrus, you have no chance.' Look at what happened. If you had to bet money where are you going to make more progress, would you have said college presidents or billionaire business people? For fifteen years we've been the social conscience of the NFL." Mehri attributes the rule's appeal to its simplicity. "It's a very modest step."

But, like other diversity initiatives, the Rooney Rule's success ultimately relies on the goodwill of the teams and the accountability provided by the league. Results on both scores appear mixed. In 2003, Tagliabue fined Detroit Lion's president and CEO Matt Millen $200,000 for violating the rule when the team hired a White coach without interviewing any candidates of color. "It was your responsibility to ensure that you and the Lions organization met the commitment or demonstrated to this office that it was impossible to meet for some justifiable reason," Tagliabue wrote in a letter to Millen.[16] Tagliabue said future violations would result in a fine of at least $500,000 for "conduct detrimental" to the league. Since then, no other team has been fined.

However, there have been other suspected violations. For example, in 2018 the Oakland Raiders came under scrutiny when it hired Jon Gruden to a ten-year, $100 million contract. Critics contended that minority candidates were not given serious consideration. Jason Reid, a sportswriter for *The Undefeated*, was among the commentators to cry foul. "Yet another NFL owner has given the middle finger, and it's time to significantly strengthen the Rooney Rule, or scrap it all together."[17] Reid noted that the rule can be easily skirted by holding casual talks with a minority member of the team's coaching staff or by bringing in a coach from another team for show to meet the letter, if not the spirit, of the rule. Concerns about sham interviews had been raised early on as the league worked with team owners to respond to Mehri and Cochran's report.

The Fritz Pollard Alliance called for an investigation of the Raiders coach hiring. The group contended that the team had only interviewed minority candidates after the decision to hire Gruden had already been made. But an NFL investigation determined that the Raiders had not violated the rule. "We strongly disagree with the NFL's conclusion," the alliance countered. "We believe the facts overwhelmingly point in the other direction. In his enthusiasm to hire Jon Gruden, Oakland Raiders' owner Mark Davis failed to fulfill his obligation . . . and should step forward and acknowledge he violated the Rule." The alliance called for a meeting with the league "to ensure a process like this never happens again."[18]

Pash conceded that the appearances were less than ideal but insisted that the two minority candidates—one the team's tight end coach and another a USC offensive coach—had been interviewed by Reggie McKenzie, who is African American and was the team's general manager until his firing in December 2018. "The interviews that were conducted were long, serious, substantive and conducted by Reggie McKenzie," Pash said. "You'd have to assume he was allowing himself to be used as some sort of scam."[19] Given Gruden's record, he said, "it's not surprising he's someone people would have an interest in."

Moreover, Pash said the Raiders club is owned by a family with a proven commitment to diversity. In addition to McKenzie, the team had hired as head coach Hall of Famer Art Shell, who was the league's first African American head coach in six decades; Thomas Flores, one of the league's first Hispanic coaches; and Amy Trask, the league's first female CEO. In 2018, Kelsey Martinez became the team's first female assistant coach. "You can't ignore people's history."

Still, in response to the criticism, the NFL agreed to tighten Rooney Rule loopholes. Under the amended rule, all candidates will have to be interviewed by the team's final decision maker—an indication that the person is being seriously considered—and the candidate must be deemed viable, meaning the person's résumé would have to be commensurate with the role of a head

NFL coach. Critics, among them the Fritz Pollard Alliance, were concerned that teams were flouting the rule by conducting sham interviews with minorities who, given their minimal experience, did not merit serious consideration. Pash said that the league's career advisory panel maintains statistical data on potential candidates and sends clubs a list of qualified contenders. "Clubs are required to interview at least one person on that list," he said, noting that it has incorporated the Fritz Pollard Alliance's list. "That wasn't the case before. We know that the interview is with a candidate who has been vetted and deemed of having the requisite experience and skills."

"You have to interview someone outside your staff unless it's a viable candidate," Mehri adds. "You can't just walk down the hall."[20]

Pash said that the amended rule requiring the key decision maker to interview all candidates and remain involved throughout the hiring process will alleviate a perception problem created when one candidate is interviewed by the most senior person and another is not.

Pash reiterated that the rule was not imposed on the teams but was adopted on their own. "When it comes right down to it, teams want to win. Sometimes, they'll hire players you wish they didn't because they have a lot of baggage. I think the same is true with coaches. I think they really do want the right coach. They frequently fail. I doubt that anyone has focused on whether the winning coach is white or black. I think we're past that."[21]

However, the NFL could do more. It's the insidiousness of unconscious racial bias that make policies like the Rooney Rule necessary to begin with. And N. Jeremi Duru, the alliance cocounsel, American University law professor, and author of *Advancing the Ball: Race, Reformation and the Quest for Equal Coaching Opportunity in the NFL*, said the group tried, but failed, to get the league to expand the rule to apply to offensive coordinators, who are often tapped for head coaching positions.

"That's your pipeline," said Duru in reference to the offensive coordinator position. "They're disproportionately and overwhelmingly White. If the Rooney Rule is not going to apply to offensive coordinators, there have to be other initiatives to strengthen the pipeline. There should be full mentorship programs for current quarterbacks."[22]

Pash pointed out that owners are not willing to surrender the autonomy of their coaches. "Very, very few head coaches have any interest in having that rule imposed on them. Their success as a head coach depends on who they get in that coordinator position."[23]

Given the historic exclusion of Blacks and other people of color, Duru fears that many former players who should be considered for head coaching jobs will simply explore other opportunities. "Maybe it's not worth it. If you managed your wealth, you don't have to do it," Duru said. "There are so many more options for someone who's played in the league."[24]

Duru has been frustrated at times by perceived violations of the rule—including 2013, when fifteen coaching and front office positions were filled by White men—but he argues that the Rooney Rule has undoubtedly created more opportunity for Blacks and other coaches of color. While he'd like to see the rule apply to a greater number of front office positions, he is pleased with the number of women, including African American women, working in the league's Park Avenue office.

Still, while the rule has placed the NFL under far greater scrutiny and resulted in more head coaches of color, since 2005 the number has never exceeded eight, and in the 2018 season, with the firing of five African American coaches, it was down to three, two of them Black and one Latino, before the Miami Dolphins hired Brian Flores, raising the number to four. Mehri argues that it has been difficult to sustain momentum over the course of sixteen years, but he believes that it has succeeded in creating equal opportunity 90 percent of the time.

With eight head coach vacancies in 2019, the NFL was once again tested. But by early 2019, seven of the eight open positions were filled by White coaches. If none are of color, "it would be a bad look," Duru said.[25]

Pash said such a scenario is unlikely. "Every coach is interviewing at least one and probably multiple" candidates of color, he said, reiterating that each club is given a list that includes viable candidates, including those on the Fritz Pollard Alliance list. However, the 2019 season began with just one general manager of color and three coaches of color in a league where nearly 70 percent of the players are Black. Four of the six coaches fired right before the 2018 season ended were of color. It remained to be seen if any would be rehired by another team during the season.

Pash maintains that the Rooney Rule, while imperfect, has been impactful. "It's made a difference in our league that's been valuable and important and I think over time it will continue to be a valuable part of what we do."[26] Mehri, meanwhile, sees the Rooney Rule as a process, not a numerical solution. "We're not asking for a leg up. Just give us a level playing field. At least we have a plan for progress."[27]

TURMOIL IN THE TRENCHES

Tanya Odom has spent the past quarter century building a global reputation as a leading diversity consultant, but nothing prepared her for the mounting stress and demand for her services since 2015. "I'm always on call; I'm emotionally drained," said Odom, a senior consultant at the FutureWork Institute, which has offices in New York, London, and Asia and whose US clients have included American Express, 3M, Goldman Sachs, and Starbucks.

"The last two years under Trump have been more stressful," she said of a racially charged tenure exacerbated by a series of high-profile events, including the shooting of nine Blacks in Charlottesville, college protests, and the "Me Too" and "Black Lives Matter" movements that have turned workplaces into tinderboxes.[1] Odom spends more time than ever doing onsite troubleshooting and fielding calls from institutions ill prepared to address race. "They don't have the racial literacy," said Odom, who is Latina and holds bachelor's and master's degrees in anthropology and education from Vassar and Harvard, respectively. "I get a ton of calls to talk about how people are feeling. I'm not a therapist but don't shy away from conversations about race and privilege. What they look for are people able to have those conversations."

While most major institutions—and at least half of Fortune 500 companies—mandate bias training, what qualifications and outcomes institutions expect of diversity professionals are often unclear. Odom had recently been approached about a diversity job in which the ad specifically required marketing and communications experience, but "nothing about global awareness, nothing about assessment skills. They don't know and they think it's about communication."

The crisis-driven workload, heightened demand, and often-vague set of desired job qualifications and expected outcomes are only among the myriad problems plaguing the growing field of diversity consultancy. These issues are exacerbated by the fact that there's been limited research or agreement on what bias reduction training is and whether it works. Moreover, there's a growing body of scholarship that suggests that much of the training mandated by thousands of companies actually does more harm than good.

"Strategies for controlling bias—which drive most diversity efforts—have failed spectacularly," Harvard professor Frank Dobbin and Tel Aviv University professor Alexandra Kalev concluded in their study "Why Diversity Programs Fail," published in the *Harvard Business Review* in 2016. Noting the lack of progress in management of Black men since 1985 and White women since 2000, they wrote: "It isn't that there aren't enough educated women and minorities out there—both groups have made huge educational gains over the past two generations. The problem is that we can't motivate people by forcing them to get with the program and punishing them if they don't."[2]

Dobbin and Kalev, both professors of sociology, examined three decades of data from more than eight hundred US firms and interviewed hundreds of managers and executives. They found that mandatory training, which they described as "command and control" approaches, don't work and often trigger a backlash, particularly among White men. Rather than being converted, they often react with anger and resistance.

A case in point is the male engineer at Google who was fired for penning a memo deriding the company's diversity efforts. He is now suing the company and characterized its subconscious bias training as "just a lot of shaming."[3]

Even more troubling is the adverse impact that mandatory training appears to have on those it is intended to help. Five years after instituting training, Dobbin and Kalev found that, on average, the number of Black women in management dropped 9.2 percent, and the numbers for Asian women and men, respectively, decreased 5.4 and 4.5 percent.[4] They also found that the grievance system, another staple in many companies, was found to have adverse effects on minorities, with their numbers actually declining by as much as 11.3 percent for Asian men and 4.1 percent for Asian women five years out. The number of Black men decreased 7.3 percent, Black women 4.8 percent, and Hispanic women 4.7 percent. Of nearly ninety thousand discrimination complaints filed with the federal Equal Employment Opportunity Commission in 2015, 45 percent of the complaints resulted in retaliation.

"Many interpreted the key learning point as having to walk on eggshells around women and minorities—choosing words carefully so as not to offend," executives Rohini Anand and Mary-Frances Winters wrote in a 2008 article on diversity training in the *Academy of Management Learning & Education*.[5] "Some surmised that it meant White men were villains, still others assumed that they would lose their jobs to minorities and women, while others concluded that women and minorities were simply too sensitive."

"Prejudice Reduction: What Works: A Review and Assessment of Research and Practice," one of the most comprehensive studies on the efficacy of diversity programs, examined 893 published and unpublished reports of interventions intended to reduce prejudice over a five-year period. The interventions included workplace diversity initiatives, multicultural education, dialogue groups, media campaigns, and cognitive training intended to combat bias related to a wide range of targets, including race, religion, age, weight, and attitudes toward diversity and multiculturalism.

According to the authors, Elizabeth Levy Paluck at Harvard's Center for International Affairs and Donald P. Green of Yale's Institution for Social and Policy Studies, "The strongest conclusion to be drawn from the field experimental literature on prejudice reduction concerns the dearth of evidence for most prejudice-reduction programs. Few programs originating in scientific laboratories, nonprofit or educational organizations, government bureaus, and consulting firms have been evaluated rigorously" they wrote, adding that "entire genres" of interventions, including organizational diversity training, advertising, cultural competence in the health and law professions, and education have not been tested.[6]

> One can argue that diversity training workshops succeed because they break down stereotypes and encourage empathy. Alternatively, one can argue that such workshops reinforce stereotypes and elicit reactance among the most prejudiced participants. Neither of these conflicting arguments is backed by the type of evidence that would convince a skeptic. . . . We currently do not know whether a wide range of programs and policies tend to work on average, and we are quite far from having an empirically grounded understanding of the conditions under which these programs work best.

Paluck and Green found that some of the field experiments examined indicated that the positive effects of diversity training at best last a day or two and even then can create backlash.[7]

Assessments of diversity training also found that programs tend to be atheoretical in both their approach and how they're evaluated. "The literature supporting diversity training is similarly lacking in theoretical rigor," argue Edna Chun and Alvin Evans in *Leading a Diversity Culture Shift in Higher Education*.[8] They cite an evaluation of 474 field studies on prejudice reduction interventions that found that 77 percent were conducted without experimental means, if evaluations were conducted at all. "When offered without clear criteria and objectives as well as a persuasive 'academic case' for their relevance, diversity education programs will fail to attain measurable, sustained impact on prevailing culture behaviors, norms or attitudes."[9]

Many of these programs grew out of Title VII of the Civil Rights Act of 1964 that made it illegal for employers with fifteen or more employees to discriminate in hiring, promotion, and training on the basis of race, color, religion, sex, and national origin. The act was later amended to prevent discrimination due to disability, sexual orientation, and pregnancy. In response to numerous lawsuits filed with the Equal Employment Opportunity Commission (EEOC), courts began mandating bias training, and in some instances courts mandated it as a remedy to findings of discrimination. Many companies began offering training proactively to avert violations and lawsuits.

While motivated by compliance, some companies, notably IBM and Xerox Corporation, early on positioned diversity as a moral imperative.[10]

One of the popular exercises employed in training sessions was the "Blue Eye/Brown Eye" experiment in which participants are separated by eye color and told that the people with brown eyes were smarter and better than those with blue eyes. The experiment was developed in 1968 by third-grade teacher Jane Elliott to teach her all-White students the arbitrariness of prejudice. As part of the experiment, she gave the children with brown eyes more privileges. She detected that the students with brown eyes became more confident and condescending, while the blue-eyed children became despondent and more timid. The widely lauded experiment demonstrated how prejudice was a learned behavior that can be unlearned.

By the 1980s, companies began promoting diversity as critical to the organization's bottom line, but by then Reagan administration deregulation policies—particularly the scuttling of EEOC conciliation agreements that set goals and timetables for increasing representation in companies—took the pressure off diversity efforts, and in some instances they came to a halt.

However, in the late 1980s and early 1990s, support for diversity rose again. In part, the renewed interest can be attributed to the 1987 release of *Workforce 2000: Work and Workers for the 21st Century*, an influential study published by the Hudson Institute. The study, which became a bestseller, highlighted population projections and an aging White population and burgeoning non-White population that by 2000 would force companies to increasingly rely on women and minorities in the workplace. The report noted the "ever-rising skill requirements of the emerging economy" and added "the task of fully utilizing minority workers [is] particularly urgent between now and 2000. Both cultural changes and education and training investments will be needed to create real equal employment opportunity."[11]

The report is credited with adding the term *workforce diversity* to the business vernacular and providing an important rationale for creating a diversity infrastructure—namely, that the labor force was becoming more diverse and that companies should adapt.[12] That, along with a number of high-profile discrimination lawsuits throughout the 1990s and 2000s, including the ones at Coca-Cola and Texaco, once again kicked diversity efforts into high gear. Companies started hosting a profusion of job fairs and other initiatives intended to increase the numbers of underrepresented minorities and women on their staffs. With the increased focus on diversity came the virulent backlash in the form of commentary and lawsuits that continue to reverberate today.

While the results of diversity efforts didn't live up to the public pronouncements, many White Americans began to sense that the nation had done enough to remedy sins of the past. Some thirty states considered nullifying their affirmative action policies, led by successful efforts in California and Washington State. The courts have significantly limited the scope of affirmative action policies, even though many institutions have continued to initiate diversity programs that no longer specifically target historically disadvantaged racial groups.

Today respect for difference of all kinds has overshadowed race and has helped maintain the systemic underrepresentation of people of color who in addition face discrimination due to their gender, LGBTQ identity, physical and mental incapacity, and class. In 2017, Denise Young Smith, Apple's first-ever vice president of inclusion and diversity, took this ever-broadening definition of diversity to its seemingly logical conclusion when, on a panel on diversity, she suggested that twelve blue-eyed blond White men could also illustrate diversity due to their different backgrounds. When asked whether she would focus on underrepresented minorities and specifically Black women, Smith, who is Black, responded: "I focus on everyone. Diversity is the human experience. I get a little bit frustrated when diversity or the term *diversity* is tagged to the people of color, or the women, or the LGBT."[13]

While the audience seemed to respond positively, Young Smith's comments were widely panned back in the United States. In an email to Apple employers, she wrote, "I regret the choice of words I used to make this point. I and understand why some people took offense. My comments were not representative of how I think about diversity or Apple sees it."[14] Within months, she had left her position.

While Coca-Cola's global chief diversity officer, Steve Bucherati said he had the distinction, at least for a time, of being the only straight White male chief diversity officer in the Fortune 500. He explained that his condition for taking the job was having access, influence, and authority. "I needed the authority to say things. There are organizations where people have all three. I know many colleagues—women and people of color—who have the same gravitas. It's their leadership."[15]

Bucherati holds a dim view of the diversity profession overall, though. "Ninety-nine percent of them are just not effective," he said of diversity chiefs and consultants. "They're academic, esoteric. Most diversity consultants have never done this inside a business with all of the complexity of budgets, bureaucracy, politics—all of this stuff that gets in the way. It's unfortunate that they are very good at marketing. There are diversity consultants out there making a fortune."

Bucherati recalled a mandatory three-day training session with an outside consultant at Coca-Cola arranged after the discrimination lawsuit was filed. "This is how that class begins: 'In the jungle, there are elephants and giraffes. They are very different but they must get along.' I wanted to shove my finger down my throat. You don't want to be there. That has zero traction. People check the box." As global chief diversity officer at Coca-Cola, he identified an effective program that focused on civil treatment as opposed to just race. "It speaks about everybody in the workplace. The civil way to behave." He said the program provided specific examples of ways to avoid bias against LGBTQ people, racial minorities, and women in the workplace.

Bucherati is now a diversity consultant himself, who begins his presentation by showing a slide of the front-page *New York Times* headline on the lawsuit filing. "I tell people don't become Coca-Cola 1999/2000. You have a chance to do this affirmatively and proactively. Some companies listen and pay attention, some don't ... You have many, many where it's for image. Some just want to do it to check the box."

Dobbin and Kalev in their work state that among the effective strategies to increase diversity is the hiring of diversity managers and the formation of task forces to monitor progress and hold the institutions accountable. They pointed to Coca-Cola as an example. "Task forces are the trifecta of diversity programs. In addition to promoting accountability, they engage members who might have previously been cool to diversity projects and increase contact among the women, minorities, and white men who participate. They pay off, too: On average, companies that put in diversity task forces see 9% to 30% increases in the representation of white women and of each minority group in management over the next five years."[16] They also noted the effectiveness of mentoring programs and the targeted recruiting of underrepresented groups, initiatives that most of the companies they examined failed to pursue.

And while they found mandatory training ineffective, they said voluntary training and cooperative ventures that bring together a diverse group to problem-solve bear results. In their study on prejudice reduction, Paluck and Green noted the benefits of cooperative ventures but also highlighted the old-fashioned intervention of reading and discussion. While not always conducive to work environments, the strategy of readings and discussion hold great promise for the classroom. "Although media, reading, and other forms of narrative and normative communication are not currently considered cutting-edge approaches, we point to the apparent success of this technique in the real world and to its potential for reducing prejudice through narrative persuasion, social norms, empathy, perspective taking, and extended contact. The persuasive and positive influence of peers (indirectly via observation or directly via discussion) is a promising area of prejudice reduction supported by laboratory research."[17]

Another study of fifty-three research assistants in a large university found post-training of skill-based diversity programs was affected by the perceived environmental consequences of supervisors and peers.[18] So the training must matter to those at the top.

Many of these studies have brought heightened scrutiny to this field and those who toil in it while deflecting attention from the leadership vacuum that has left diversity professionals holding the bag. While they work in the trenches and are held to account for workplace tensions and uninspiring results, many critics ignore the extent to which their success—or that of any initiative they deploy—wholly rests on the will, intention, and competence of those at the top of the institutions they serve.

In spite of the criticism leveled at her profession, the debates over protocols, the varying skill level of practitioners, and the questionable effectiveness of training, Odom said she has witnessed change. "Organizations are having real conversations; they're having to look in the mirror. Diversity initiatives may not show progress right away. The focus has to be as much on the culture as who's there. It has to be more holistic than it's been. You can't talk about diversity and not speak about what's happening on the outside."[19]

Most of her private sector work entails working closely with chief diversity officers who, she said, when strategic, effect change. But some have no awareness of the Civil Rights Movement, while others "want to be the sage on the stage" rather than do the difficult work to drive change. "This space is flooded with people doing this work," she said, while noting many work in a vacuum, without tying the work to its historical context. "We're not very good at knowing history."

Beyond conducting assessments and helping set up systems of accountability, her work chiefly entails listening. While conducting assessments on a college campus, employees of color told her how beaten down and undervalued they and their students felt. In a corporate setting, a Black employee was upset about a colleague who wore a MAGA hat to work. "I'm concerned about the people who stay in corporate America—what it has done to them. Women of color who constantly look over their shoulders while constantly dealing with things on the outside."[20]

Odom is also struck by the burdens placed on chief diversity officers who must straddle the internal and external pressures of the job, often with little support from human resources. Many are from underrepresented minority groups and are typically the most senior people of color in their organizations. And their prestigious titles often belie the limited resources they are allocated or clout they wield within their organizations. "A lot is put on them," Odom said, which over time often leads to risk aversion, disillusion, and burnout.

"We're treated like fire extinguishers," Bribiescas at Yale said of diversity officers. "After things die down the mentality is 'we'll call on you when there's another crisis.' You have to change fundamental aspects of the culture but we're averse to uncomfortable conversations."[21] Noting the stress of the job and the undervaluing of the work, Bribiescas said during meetings of diversity officers across the country, "agendas go out the window and they become therapy sessions."

The experiences Bribiescas and Odom described are backed up by the research Chun and Evans did for their influential book *Leading a Diversity Culture Shift in Higher Education*. They surveyed chief diversity officers and conducted in-depth interviews with thirty-two of them from schools around the country. Chun said the sensitivity of the issue and the fragility of their often-untenured positions leaves many hesitant to speak about problems on their campuses. "There's also a structural problem in institutions where the overwhelming majority of chief diversity officers are of color and the other executives and employees are overwhelmingly White. The structure still is a White male hierarchy; most provosts are White males, most presidents. Most of the highest positions. It's a form of tokenism. Diverse people on the frontlines are experiencing day to day what it means to work in predominantly White institutions."[22]

While a growing number of diversity officers in universities have doctorate degrees, which helps establish their credibility, most are untenured, leaving them vulnerable in environments where their presence, and the issues they raise, are typically unwelcome. "When an employee serves at will he or she can be let go for anything. They know that. We've seen a lot of turnover in diversity officers. It's not popular. They cannot do it without tenure. It is difficult to be effective."

Chun observed that one of the most difficult constituencies to bring on board for diversity in higher education is the faculty. Part of it is due to their resistance to "training," which she agrees doesn't work. She said diversity initiatives should be led by faculty and linked to the discipline. Beyond that, diversity officers struggle to establish links with the university community without a mandate of change from the top and to find ways to tiptoe through the minefield of race and gender by "framing it in terms of a non-blaming framework. To describe it in ways that don't alienate people."[23]

There are other hurdles diversity officers face while striving to do their jobs effectively. Chun argues that changing the culture "should be competency-based and linked to specific desired outcomes," meaning training is not one-size-fits-all but is adapted to the environment and institutional needs. Moreover, she cited a survey of 771 chief diversity officers that found that 63 percent had difficulty even arriving at a common definition for diversity on their campus. This difficulty often leaves the goals, like the term, opaque. The wide spectrum can range from valuing difference to social justice for those who have been historically excluded and disadvantaged. The same survey found that only one-third of diversity education and training programs were directed to senior administrators compared to 43 percent faculty and 51 percent staff and 50 percent students.[24]

As the former chair of Yale's anthropology department, Bribiescas is tenured but said he feels protective of staff members working on diversity who are not. "When we meet with senior leadership, I'm mindful of people who don't have tenure who are professionally vulnerable. People who work in diversity and inclusion are not doing any favors to their professional development. There's data that if you engage, it's detrimental to your career."[25]

In one such study, researchers surveyed 350 executives on whether they respected cultural, religious, gender, and racial differences and valued and felt comfortable working with a diverse group. Diversity-valuing behavior was not found to benefit the executives in terms of how they were rated. However, women and non-White executives who valued diversity received adverse ratings. "Participants rated nonwhite managers and female managers as less effective when they hired a nonwhite or female job candidate instead of a white male candidate," the authors Stefanie K. Johnson and David R. Hekman wrote in the article "Women and Minorities Are Penalized for Promoting Diversity."[26] "High status groups, mainly white men, are given freedom to deviate from the status quo because their competence is assumed based on their membership in the high status group."

As a result of perceived consequences, women and minorities may choose not to advocate for other women and minorities. This kind of risk aversion may explain why Apple's former diversity officer equated the myriad perspectives of blond, blue-eyed White men with efforts to expand opportunities for underrepresented minorities and women. The study also showed that non-White applicants who include experience related to their ethnicity on their résumés are more likely to be passed over for jobs.

These potential occupational hazards, Chun explained, mean that committed leadership is critical. "They're change agents," she said of diversity professionals. "Change is difficult, and you have to have institutional leadership that spearheads that change." Leaders, she said, "have to survive a lot of winds that are buffeting them."[27]

Among those headwinds are efforts to defund or downsize diversity programs at a number of state universities, including the Universities of Tennessee and Nebraska. In Tennessee, state representative James "Micah" Van Huss, a Republican, sponsored legislation to defund the University of Tennessee's Office of Diversity and Inclusion in response to guidelines over gender-neutral pronouns and holiday parties. "First it was Sex Week, then the Gender Neutral Pronoun," he said in a statement. "Now these recommendations to ensure that 'holiday' parties have nothing to do with Christmas. What else has the Office of Diversity been doing with our tax dollars?"[28]

Two other legislators called for the resignation of the university chancellor, Jimmy Cheek. "The Office of Diversity is not welcoming to all and hostile to none as they claim," state senator Dolores Gresham, the Republican chair of the Education Committee, said in a statement. "They are very hostile to students and other Tennesseans with Christian and conservative values."[29]

Jimmy Duncan, a Republican member of Congress, weighed in, saying: "People from all over the country are sick and tired of all this extreme, radical political correctness."[30]

In response, Cheek, a Texan-born Asian American, said: "I am disappointed that our efforts to be more inclusive have been totally misconstrued." He said he sought to "promote ways to be inclusive of all cultures and religions."[31] Cheek survived the controversy, but the Office of Diversity did not. In 2016, legislation passed to disband it and eliminate four staff positions. The bill stipulated that no state funds could be used for the office, which was mostly state funded. The state funds were reallocated to sponsor, for one year, scholarships for minority students in engineering programs. A month later, Cheek announced his resignation, effective upon the hiring of his successor. He said his decision was unrelated to the controversy. He stepped down in 2017 at age seventy, having overseen the major expansion of the university during his eight-year tenure.

Diversity funding was also under attack in Nebraska, where in 2018 a state senator criticized the search for the university's first vice chancellor for diversity. In a letter to his constituents posted on the Nebraska legislature website, Sen. Steve Erdman said once that person is hired, "every word spoken by White Christian conservative males at the school will be excruciatingly scrutinized against the backdrop of the new Vice Chancellor's extremist progressive worldview."[32] He continued, "Recent Left-wing movements, such as Black Lives Matter and #MeToo, have undoubtedly put tremendous pressure upon the administration to do more about diversity and inclusion." While "nobody I know advocates for racial, gender or sexual orientation discrimination," the new position would "impose favoritism" upon those groups. He went on to baselessly claim that the position would lead to the hiring of unqualified faculty, adding that the new chancellor would now mandate diversity "regardless of talent, education, experience, or expertise in the field."

This backlash, of course, intensifies the pressure on already-struggling diversity officers. Chun and Odom echoed Bollinger's concern that diversity initiatives have been isolated from history and the unfinished civil rights struggle for African Americans and other racial minorities. "It began with affirmative action policies, which were scuttled by the Supreme Court," said Chun. "Now the Supreme Court said the only thing we can talk about is diversity. The reinterpretation has left us with diversity for everybody. It's something that can be added on that you don't necessarily have to have. There's probably not a real desire to have something happen anyway. It relates to power. People don't want to change. They want the status quo."[33]

While many recent studies raise legitimate concerns about diversity practices, most have overshadowed the extent to which these initiatives ceased to be seen as a moral imperative linked to centuries of systemic racial oppression. Moreover, the emphasis on metrics suggests that justice and equality can be neatly quantified. Metrics are inevitably used to show the economic impact of diversity on companies while neglecting to show the economic impact of injustice and inequality on the nation's overtaxed criminal justice and health care systems. How can one quantify the toll the lack of opportunity or underemployment has taken on individuals' broken lives?

To effect change, leaders of institutions, whether corporate executives or university presidents, must contend with a society that has historically devalued—or outright disparaged—racial diversity and inclusion. But it is left to leaders to set the tone for workplaces that often marginalize those to whom diversity initiatives fall. Countless institutions have hired chief diversity officers and commissioned task forces that have felled forests with mountain of reports that have been promptly filed away and forgotten. "Everybody is quick to do unconscious bias training and not interventions," said Mehri. "It's about looking like you're doing something. They want drive-by diversity. If diversity and inclusion is buried in the organizational structure it's not going to have a lot of power. When you keep choosing the options on the menu that don't create change you're purposely not creating change. It's part of the intentional discrimination."[34]

Pamela Coukos, Mehri's law partner, said resistance to fresh approaches undermines progress. "We're real attached to the way we're making decisions. It's kind of complicity. We're ok with the 'if onlys.'"[35]

The best efforts of diversity professionals are bound to fail without a true commitment to institutional transformation. A leader's ability to translate that commitment to his or her team in ways that inspire, rather than shame, epitomizes leadership.

"It's got to come from the top. No question about that," said former University of Missouri interim president Michael Middleton. "The president can write the script and figure out what the office needs to be successful. The president has to be the one to say this is what we're doing; this is what we're about."[36] He said the $7 million he allocated for diversity at the University of Missouri could only bear fruit if leadership is committed to change. Otherwise, he said, "all the university is going to do is come up with some training programs, hiring programs, the standard stuff everyone's been doing the last few decades. And it hasn't really worked. Success can't be measured by the amount of money you spend on it."

CHAPTER
9

DIVERSITY, INC.

"Not everything that is faced can be changed, but nothing can be changed until it is faced."
—James Baldwin

Decades after *diversity* became a buzzword in the workplace, the business promoting its virtue and profitability is booming. From the rise in online diversity courses, professional organizations, magazines, training sessions, national conferences, and job postings, to the high-profile hiring of corporate czars and establishment of degree programs at prestigious schools, the lucrative industry is thriving, even if diversity is not.

As early as 2003, MIT professor Thomas Kochan estimated that companies were spending upward of $8 billion a year on diversity efforts but that the industry "is built on sand."[1] In the years since Trump's 2016 election, the diversity industry has exploded. In March 2018, the job site Indeed.com reported that postings for diversity and inclusion jobs had risen a whopping 35 percent in the previous two years. The number had increased 18 percent over the previous year, with 130 per million job postings seeking diversity and inclusion professionals. During the fifteen months before Trump's election, eighty-seven of every one million jobs were for diversity and inclusion roles.

A 2019 survey of 234 companies in the S&P 500— 47 percent of which had diversity professionals—found that 63 percent had been appointed or promoted to their roles in the past three years. The survey results were reported in *A Leader's Guide: Finding and Keeping Your Next Chief Diversity Officer*, by the global search and leadership consulting firm Russell Reynolds Associates.[2]

Among the high-profile companies and institutions that were advertising for diversity officers were Ogilvy, Estee Lauder, and American Express. In 2018, Netflix joined the growing list of companies to hire its first-ever executive to focus on diversity and inclusion after the chief communications officer was fired for using the N-word in the workplace. Uber, the ride-sharing company, also hired its first diversity officer in the wake of charges of sexual discrimination. Among the others hiring their first diversity czars were the NFL, Gucci, and Prada. Each publicized workplace scandal brings fresh opportunities for the industry's growth.

The ascendance of the industry has been marked by the establishment of diversity degree and certification programs at universities, some of which themselves appear in need of diversity assistance. Tufts University offers a graduate-level master of art degree in diversity and inclusion leadership. The tuition for a master's at Tufts for the 2018/2019 academic year was $51,288, suggesting that prospective students believe it a worthy investment. Tufts's literature noted, "To be an effective leader in diversity and inclusion you must understand the social contexts and psychological processes that result in implicit bias, discrimination and marginalization." But according to its fall 2017 data, Tufts University's faculty was just 2.6 percent Black/African American, 11.4 percent Asian, and 4.2 percent Hispanic "of any race." Among its undergraduate student body, 4.1 percent was Black, 11.9 percent Asian, and 6.8 percent Hispanic "of any race." Another 4.9 percent was two or more races, and 5.4 percent "Race/Ethnicity unknown."[3]

Cornell and Georgetown Universities were also among the schools that offered a certificate program in diversity and inclusion. Cornell offered courses in equal employment opportunity law, talent management, and strategies for advancing diversity and inclusion. The cost for a three-day seminar in 2019 was $1,995, and a two-day workshop on the fundamentals of diversity and inclusion was offered for $1,495. Tuition for the Georgetown certificate was $7,500 for a total of six courses. At Cornell, for fall 2018, the faculty was 74.9 percent White, 8.1 percent underrepresented minority, and 11.3 percent "other minority."[4] Georgetown's faculty was far more diverse, with Blacks and Asians proportionally represented at 13.4 percent and 6.3 percent, respectively. But Hispanics/Latinx, while 18 percent of the national population, held 5.1 percent of faculty positions.

The Russell Reynolds survey found that diversity professionals working in the S&P 500 came from a variety of fields, including human resources, law/compliance, communications, and business. About half previously served in diversity and inclusion roles.

More than half of the surveyed professionals said they do not have the resources or support needed to execute programs and strategies, and only 35 percent had access to company demographic metrics, which, as the Coca-Cola case showed, is the most effective way to drive change and compliance. And tellingly, all of the eighteen hundred–plus company managers surveyed ranked diversity last on a list of eight potential company priorities.

Still, as the field expands attempts to professionalize it and standardize the training have resulted in countless offline and online programs devoted to diversity training. One, the Diversity Executive Leadership Academy, offers programs leading to certifications, including CDE (Cultural Diversity Executive) and CDP (Certified Diversity Professional).

The nonprofit National Diversity Council, which describes itself as "the national voice for diversity," in 2015 launched DiversityFIRST, a five-day intensive certification program that promised to "put you at the forefront of this exciting and rewarding profession."[5] Graduates would be recognized as Certified Diversity Professionals (CDPs), which, given debates over training methodology, efficacy, and resources in the workplace, raises questions about the degree to which the certification will enable graduates to effectuate change in the workplace. However, in a field based on impressions, the credentials may help graduates secure employment in the flourishing field, particularly given the imprimatur of the council's elite program partners—among them American Express, AT&T, and Morgan Stanley. The council graduated its first class of twenty-three

CDPs in 2015 and by 2019 was offering courses in ten cities, including Chicago, Atlanta, and Dallas.

There is an ever-growing number of national diversity organizations targeted to specific fields, including law, higher education, and library science, with conferences drawing thousands of diversity professionals to cities around the country to discuss the latest trends in the field. In 2019 alone, national conferences included the 23rd Annual Diversity & Inclusion Conference in Brooklyn hosted by the Conference Board; the two-day Inclusive Diversity Conference in San Francisco, where speakers would examine, among other topics, the science of diversity; and the Diversity and Inclusion Conference and Exposition, hosted in New Orleans by the Society for Human Resource Management, which claims a global network of three hundred thousand professionals. The National Association of Diversity Officers in Higher Education was holding its annual conference in Philadelphia. Registration for the conferences ranged from $500 to $2,400 (not including hotel, meals, and travel) and promised to generate millions of dollars for the host cities.

In addition to departments in major law firms devoted to diversity consulting, an ever-growing number of firms are tapping into the market to guide companies through the rocky terrain. Cyrus Mehri and his partner, Pamela Coukos, have leveraged their experience suing companies such as Coca-Cola and Texaco to launch Working Ideal, a company that specializes in diversity, inclusion and equity assessments, workplace harassment, pay equity audits, and leadership development. April Reign, a former campaign finance lawyer who launched #OscarsSoWhite, now works full time as a consultant to the film industry.

There is also an ever-growing number of large global companies devoted to diversity, including CSOFT International, which specializes in cultural expertise, regulatory compliance, and document translation and employs more than 450 people and 10,000 contractors.

In 2019, former American Bar Association president Hilarie Bass left her firm to start the nonprofit Bass Institute for Diversity & Inclusion to address the paucity of women and racial minorities across industries. The same year, Michelle Silverthorn left her position as diversity and education director at the Illinois Supreme Court Commission on Professionalism to launch Inclusion Nation, a diversity and education consulting firm.

There is no shortage of journals and magazines devoted to the issue, including the former *Black Issues in Higher Education*, which changed its name to *Diverse Issues in Higher Education* "to more accurately reflect its comprehensive news coverage of diversity and inclusion issues in higher education."[6] There are diversity blogs and books and boot camps and best practices. There are innumerable journals, job sites, targeted grants, and websites. There's even a Diversity and Inclusion Index (D&I Index), created in 2016 by Thomson Reuters, a multinational mass media and information firm, to assess the practices of more than seven thousand publicly traded companies globally and to recognize the top one hundred.

Conspicuously lacking, however, is diversity. This, despite decades of public pledges and the development of pricy apparatuses that have resulted, at best, in incremental progress addressing the pervasive exclusion of racial minorities on corporate boards, in executive suites, in Hollywood studios, and before college classrooms. While many in and entering the burgeoning industry may be well meaning, the same can no longer be said for many of the institutions they seek to change. In most instances, the sobering statistics can no longer be attributed to the pipeline, given the tens of thousands of people of color with advanced degrees or who otherwise have the requisite skills to produce, curate, coach, instruct, act, direct, dance, create, lead.

Clarence Otis, the former CEO of Darden, attributed the slow rate of progress in many industries—including higher education, Hollywood, the arts, and tech—to a combination of nepotism, elitism, and amateurishness. He characterized the least diverse fields as creative or boutique and noted that they are far more likely to bypass basic business principles and more inclined to engage in nepotism and cronyism, which undermine diversity.

He added that fields such as investment banking and law are small enough to forgo basic business principles and rely on a smaller network of associates to fill positions.

"They are not professionally managed," Otis said. Many lack clearly defined job descriptions and roles with compensation tiers—from the entry level through senior management—along with job-posting requirements, anti-nepotism rules, and other procedures that promote fairness and equality. "Many young, small and/or very high growth companies don't have this basic foundation. They preserve opportunities for family and cronies. Other industries have gotten past the amateurishness." He noted that publicly traded companies require senior leaders to disclose "related party" transactions—including the salaries of employees who are close relatives. "This is basic scientific management."[7]

Best practice companies, he said, layer in diversity by requiring diverse candidate slates for hiring and promotions and integrating diversity into every aspect of their business.

Like Harvard's Dobbin, Otis contends the pipeline is no longer the issue. "They have a problem because they haven't approached it with sophisticated management. It's not that complicated. It's intentionality. How serious are you? It's not rocket science."

To illustrate how the number of people in the pipeline is not resulting in comparable opportunity, the Leadership Council on Legal Diversity said that 32 percent of first-year law students are of color, compared to 23 percent who are associates, 8 percent who are partners, and 6 percent who are equity partners.[8]

While the number of CEOs of color at Fortune 500 companies has declined, representation of people of color in many companies nearly matches their proportion of the population.

In 2016, in the last report of the EEOC, Blacks, Hispanics/Latinx, and Asians comprised roughly 36 percent of the workforce. They also held about 22.2 percent of midlevel management positions and 13.7 percent of executive-level positions.[9]

At large corporations, Otis said, "the fight for talent is exhausting. Millennials are like, 'Bye, I'll get a job elsewhere.' It's intentionality. How serious are you? If AT&T looks like this, why don't you?"

However, while more representative of the national population than other sectors, corporate America has yet to fully embrace diversity at the top. The 2016 EEOC figures also show that Whites, who were 61.38 percent of the workforce, held 85 percent of executive-level positions and were 76 percent of midlevel managers.

Fortune 500 boards remain overwhelmingly White and male. "Missing Pieces Report: The 2016 Board Diversity Census of Women and Minorities on Fortune 500 Boards," a multiyear study published by the Alliance for Board Diversity (ABD), in collaboration with Deloitte Company, found that 35.9 percent of Fortune 500 board seats were held by women and minorities, compared to 30.1 percent in 2010. Still, nearly 70 percent were still held by White men.[10] There had only been slight gains in the six years that the alliance had begun tracking board diversity. Among minorities, including African Americans/Blacks, Asian/Pacific Islanders, and Hispanics/Latino(a)s, the percentage had inched up from 12.8 percent in 2010 to 14.4 percent in 2016. In that time, the total number of board seats had slightly decreased from 5,463 to 5,440. There has been an 18.4 increase in women and minorities in the Fortune 100 companies, compared to 1 percent in the Fortune 500. Still, 82.5 percent of total Fortune 100 seats were held by Whites. Asian/Pacific Islanders showed continued growth, but overall representation was 3.2 percent, for a total of 38 seats. Hispanic/ Latino men lost two board seats, while Hispanic/Latina women gained four seats since 2012. Combined Hispanics held fifty-four seats, or 5 percent, showing them to be the most disproportionately underrepresented.

The report said at the current rate of progress the organization would not achieve its target of 40 percent women and minority before 2026.

"This is not acceptable," said Ronald C. Parker, then chair of the ABD and former president and CEO of the Executive Leadership Council. "We are looking at an entire decade of virtually no growth. If other business objectives yielded the same results, it would be viewed as unacceptable business performance."[11]

The report also indicated that women and minorities were more likely than White men to serve on multiple boards, with African Americans appearing to have the highest rate of recycling, "indicating that companies are going to the same individuals rather than expanding the pool of African American/Black candidates for board membership," Parker said.[12]

In twelve years, between 2004 and 2016, the percentage of minority men on Fortune 100 boards has only increased 1 percent. "A great deal of work remains for corporate board composition to keep pace with the changing demographics of the country at large," Parker said.[13]

Linda Akutagawa, CEO and president of Leadership Education for Asian Pacifics, Inc. (LEAP), said stereotypes of Asian and Pacific Islanders as "doers and not leaders" results in them being excluded from the leadership pipeline and board positions. She challenged companies to reenvision what leaders look like, while Cid Wilson, president and CEO of the Hispanic Association on Corporate Responsibility (HACR) also lamented the slow rate of progress for Hispanics.

The 2018 "Missing Pieces" report showed that Whites occupied 83.9 percent of Fortune 500 and 80.5 percent of Fortune 100 seats.[14] That compares to 85.6 percent and 82.5 percent, respectively, in 2016.

Mehri said one has only to look at areas where wealth is created to find the wall obstructing racial progress. "If you want to create diversity you have to get companies to expose top compensation and you will see that's where the exclusion is."[15]

Mehri said bodies like the Securities Exchange Commission should require publicly traded companies to file a diversity report card to promote greater transparency and accountability.

But revelations of stark inequality in recent decades have continually failed to spark the seismic shift that's needed to fold diversity—to integrate justice—into the center of American life. They have, instead, triggered temporary fixes, public expressions of regret, and pledges that have failed to usher in enduring change. Like a game of Whac-A-Mole, the most obvious offenders get caught, while most get away.

Yet companies continue to invest billions of dollars in diversity structures. In 2014, Google alone reportedly spent $114 million on its diversity program and another $150 million in 2015. But in 2019, its fifth diversity report showed that Blacks were especially underrepresented, followed by Hispanics/Latinx. Overall, Blacks were 3.3 percent of the workforce and held 2.1 percent of tech and 2.6 percent of leadership positions. Latinx were 5.7 percent of the workforce and held 4.5 percent of tech and 3.3 of leadership roles. Meanwhile, Asians were 39.8 percent of the workforce and held 45.1 percent of tech and 28.9 percent of leadership positions; while Whites were 54.4 percent of the workforce and held 51.1 percent of tech and 66 percent of leadership positions. (Native Americans comprised .8 percent of the overall staff.) Most, if not all, of Google's one hundred thousand employees have attended a diversity workshop, but the training has not resulted in a significantly transformed workforce. In five years, the proportion of Blacks in tech roles inched up from 1.5 percent to 2.1 percent.

The initiatives at Google, of course, don't address the vast disparities outside the workplace. Black and Hispanic students face structural barriers of access and exposure to computer science. A 2016 study by Gallup and commissioned by Google found that

Black and Hispanic students are less likely than their White peers to use a computer at home or to have classes dedicated to computer science at school. "In general, when students have access to CS learning in school, they are more likely to say they are very interested in learning it—suggesting that exposure to these opportunities is key to piquing students' interest in the first place," noted the report.[16] The study also showed that 31 percent of Black, 35 percent of Hispanic, and just 21 percent of White students said they were "very interested" in learning computer science in the future. Conversely, 20 percent of White students, 16 percent of Hispanic students, and just 12 percent of Black students said they were "not at all interested" in computer science. Ninety-two percent of Black and Hispanic parents said they would like their child to learn computer science in the future. This compared to 84 percent of White parents. So for Black and Hispanic students, the issue is less interest than access.

These findings graphically show that Black and Hispanic students hunger for—but lack access to—computer science instruction. So why, then, do companies like Google, instead of investing more in the pipeline, continue to pour hundreds of millions of dollars into diversity initiatives that haven't worked? Initiatives that, as Kochan said, appear to be built on sand?

While it would be easy to dismiss many of the high-profile efforts as window dressing—as flashy public relations ploys to ameliorate tensions or take an institution out of the news—research by Lauren B. Edelman, a professor of law and sociology at UC Berkeley and the author of *Working Law: Courts, Corporations and Symbolic Civil Rights*, suggests that the multimillion-dollar initiatives may, in the end, actually be intended to save money. Edelman said that the passage of the Civil Rights Act of 1964 and other laws intended to ameliorate disadvantage had been the most significant encroachment on companies since the labor legislation of the 1930s.

In the early 1990s, following passage of the Civil Rights Act of 1991, which attempted to strengthen the earlier measure, Edelman began interviewing managers to gauge their response to it. She realized that managers were no longer speaking about affirmative action. "They were all talking about diversity. And I was talking to White men and wondered why were they all talking about diversity? That didn't comport with what I was seeing," she said, noting the overwhelmingly White composition of their staffs.[17] The observation resulted in her studying organizational responses to the Civil Rights Acts of 1964 and 1991. By reviewing the ways in which equal employment opportunity and affirmative action (EEO/AA) laws had been enforced, she sought to understand why they had not resulted in substantive change for women and minorities, who have yet to achieve parity with White males in employment or pay.

Edelman coauthored an article that explored a random sample of 1,024 federal civil rights cases decided since passage of the 1964 Civil Rights Act. She and her coauthor found that judges base company compliance on the mere presence of diversity policies, programs, or officers, without scrutinizing their efficacy.

Edelman traced the weakening of discrimination protection following the 1971 Supreme Court decision in *Griggs v. Duke Power Company,* which determined that discrimination under Title VII was based on the impact, not only the actions, of employers. However, she said courts since 1976 had narrowed the applicability of that decision by requiring plaintiffs to prove not only the impact of workplace policies or actions but also employers' *intent* to discriminate, which is far more difficult to prove. Edelman said studies consistently show that employment discrimination lawsuits are among the most difficult to win, adding that of seventy-two categories, only four had lower plaintiff win rates than did employment discrimination's 21 percent success rate. Moreover, the overwhelming majority of victims of discrimination do not even pursue legal redress.

"Therefore, although EEO/AA law does not specifically require it, organizations respond to law by creating new offices, positions, rules, and procedures . . . as visible symbols of their attention to EEO/AA issues and their efforts to comply," Edelman wrote.[18]

The formal diversity structures need not effectively decrease discrimination but rather "are symbolic gestures to public opinion, the views of constituents, social norms or law." The diversity apparatus, then, serves as shield against successful bias lawsuits that are already difficult to win.

Diversity professionals help institutionalize and legitimize the models of compliance through journals, conventions, and workshops. With the assistance of the courts, Edelman argued, these professionals rationalize the profession and the symbols of their trade. These structures, Edelman concluded, are created "largely as gestures to their legal environments" to "secure legitimacy and minimize the threat of liability." The larger and more visible the organization, and the more vulnerable they are to legal repercussions, the more resources they invest in pricy, and publicly visible, systems. "There needs to be more awareness that courts are not looking at the symbolic structures. The best we can hope for is more awareness by the judiciary. I'm not seeing any yet."[19]

Mehri said more conservative courts have only made it more difficult to prove discrimination. "It's been a failure of imagination, a failure of will," added Coukos. "It's so easy to not do it."[20]

Bari-Ellen Roberts recalls standing before the television cameras in New York on November 15, 1996, the day the landmark Texaco discrimination settlement was announced. "There were all these people with the TV cameras and microphones, this historic settlement and they were all talking about the money. Texaco lost this much on the stock market. How much fourteen hundred African Americans would receive. What irked me was nobody was talking about the discrimination. Nobody said, 'How did it feel to go to work every day and be treated as less than?' Nobody asked about how this white guy told me in a meeting on diversity with all white men, 'I'm the liberal, and I speak for you.' Nobody wants to talk about this."[21]

Roberts now works as a cancer patient advocate. In 2018 she had been in remission from stage IV cancer for eight years. "The discrimination plays on your health. It hurt Sil [Chambers] a lot more than me, and he was a young guy," she said of one of the plaintiffs in the Texaco lawsuit. Chambers was forty-three and a financial analyst at the time of the settlement and died a short time later.

Two decades later, given the attention paid to the settlement amount, rather than the cause, Roberts said, "I knew that things weren't going to change. I'm disappointed but not at all surprised."

Still, there are some on the front lines of this fight inspired by flashes of hope. Many in and outside of the art world applauded Agnes Gund, the president emerita of the Museum of Modern Art, who sold *Masterpiece*, her prized 1962 Roy Lichtenstein painting, and donated $100 million of the proceeds to fund Art For Justice to address mass incarceration and criminal justice reform.

Gund recruited other like-minded people—including the Ford Foundation's Darren Walker and former American Express CEO Kenneth Chenault and his wife, Kathy—to leverage their resources and platforms to help reduce incarceration by 20 percent in targeted high-incarceration states in five years. Gund had for years quietly brought the same renegade spirit to her private art collection, which includes artists of color alongside more widely recognized contemporary masters, helping secure them a place in the mainstream art world. While president of MOMA from 1991 to 2002, she helped engineer the inclusion of people of color on the board and is among those still pushing for significant improvement in representation of its professional staff over the next few years. "It is critical," Gund said during an interview in late 2018. "It's going slowly," she said of diversity efforts at MOMA. "I think in two years we'll reach 20 percent. It's not enough of a percentage but I think at some point it will be."[22]

Gund attributes the racial barriers in the art world and beyond to the segregated nature of American life, which, for many Whites, renders people of color virtually invisible. Gund said many Whites in her Upper East Side Manhattan social sphere don't personally know or even typically encounter African Americans. "When they do they're not really seeing them," she said. "They're not getting to know them." This invisibility informs the practices of elite institutions, which operate as if in a homogenous bubble.

But Gund's paradigm-shifting Art and Justice initiative placed the issue of racial injustice squarely in the center of the rarefied world of art and privilege, making it impossible to ignore.

In 2019, MOMA announced it was closing for four months during the summer and fall for a renovation and expansion that would change the way the museum told the story of modern art. The museum planned to more fully integrate women and people of color into its collection and exhibitions. It will reopen with exhibitions by African American artists Betye Saar and Pope L. and with a survey of Latin American art. MOMA also planned to collaborate on exhibitions with the Studio Museum in Harlem, which was also undergoing renovations.

"The museum didn't emphasize female artists, didn't emphasize what minority artists were doing," said Leon Black, the chair of MOMA's board. "Where those were always the exceptions, now they really should be part of the reality of the multicultural society we all live in."[23]

Similar omissions were also being examined by a University of Virginia Commission on Slavery and the University, which was looking for ways to partner with African Americans to address the legacy of discrimination. "It's an opportunity to partner to support the HBCU mission and help predominantly White institutions think about what we can do," Von Daacke, a cochair of the commission, said. "We stopped thinking about repair. Let's pilot programs to commit university resources to address some of this. What we haven't done is define what that is."[24]

There were also plans to unveil a prominent memorial to thousands of enslaved laborers on the University of Virginia's Charlottesville campus. Eighty feet in diameter, it will recognize the thousands of unsung enslaved African Americans whose labor contributed to the university and also memorialize

Isabella Gibbons, who had learned to read and write and after emancipation and who became the first teacher of color in the Charlottesville Freedmen's School, now the Jefferson School.

An interior polished stone wall was to bear the known names of nearly one thousand enslaved people who worked on the campus between 1817 and 1865. The total number of enslaved people is estimated at five thousand, each of whose lives will be recognized.

Von Daacke said the monument will be an overdue testament to the humanity and resistance of the unsung contributors to the school and a rare public reminder of a chapter of history that has largely remained unspoken. He said that while history cannot be undone, monuments matter if institutions are to become more inclusive of diverse populations. "Actually you can change DNA. We're still at the beginning, but you can do it. You can move people."

However, Van Daacke said institutions cannot claim a commitment to diversity and inclusion without honestly confronting and correcting destructive narratives. "If we're going to increase diversity among our student body, we have to present a different image of who we are. Diversity demands more truth-telling of our past."

By 2018, a browning America was beginning to change the meaning of mainstream in a film industry that historically catered to a White audience, or what it imagined it to be. In 2018, the number-one film was *Black Panther*, a film by a Black director featuring a Black superhero that grossed more than a billion dollars globally. *Crazy Rich Asians* (2018), a film by director Jon M. Chu and the first major motion picture in twenty-five years featuring an Asian cast, was another box office sensation.

Both films had predominantly non-White casts without so-called A-list actors and thus defied the usual formula for blockbuster films. Even the 2017 Disney animated film *Coco*, about a Mexican boy who visits the ghosts of his ancestors, outperformed popular films like *Lego Batman*. It grossed more than $800 million worldwide and went on to win two Academy Awards.

Studio executives apparently took notice. The year 2018 closed with Columbia Pictures announcing a multimillion-dollar development deal with ColorCreative, the company cofounded and owned by Issa Rae, the African American creator, writer, and star of the HBO series *Insecure*. The venture aims to develop more films by emerging and diverse filmmakers. Director Ava DuVernay's ARRAY was also added to the growing list of production companies that aimed to feed the demand for a wider range of images and voices.

In the midst of his organization's boycott of Paramount Pictures, Nogales at the National Hispanic Media Coalition acknowledged a sudden uptick in television work for Latino writers.

E. Brian Dobbins also observed an increase in opportunity for writers of color, especially on television given the expanded venues offered by cable. "We've become more data reliant. Data drives everything. The marketplace is browning. America is certainly browning, and the interest of our audience is not leaning toward movies with all White people."[25]

While the list of 2019 Academy Award nominations was characteristically panned and praised, it undoubtedly reflected a more diverse range of films and filmmakers. *Black Panther* received seven nominations and became the first superhero film nominated for Best Picture. Unlike years in which none of the Best Actor and Actress nominees were of color, in 2019 three of the top acting awards went to actors of color.

The diverse nominees would mean that April Reign could, at least temporarily, retire #OscarsSoWhite. "We've seen more diverse nominees not just with actors, but behind the camera, which is just as important," Reign said. "This is an old White institution that has been around for almost one hundred years. For it to make substantive change has been a big deal. What we saw in 2018 is this renaissance of films that reflect different facets of the [American] experience." She said while it was legitimate to ask if it marked a moment or a movement, "it's been gratifying."[26]

Still, UCLA's "Hollywood Diversity Report 2019" said that despite "notable gains" for people of color, particularly in television, "they remained underrepresented on every industry employment front."[27]

If diversity is to flower, it cannot be hermetically sealed off from the cultural ecosystem in which it is implanted. It must be rooted in a mutual understanding of our past and its profound legacy. Viewing America through rose-colored lenses has prevented most White Americans from coming to terms with the myriad ways in which race continues to pervert national ideals and undermine justice. Without truthful encounters with the past, racial reconciliation is doubtful and diversity will remain little more than a hollow abstraction.

Since the 1960s, much of the progress toward diversity has been prompted by crisis, urban unrest, public shaming like #OscarsSoWhite, social movements like "Black Lives Matter," or college protests that pierced the façade of campus tranquility.

Without these public uprisings, institutions have been slow to address enduring racial injustice that has defined the nation's history. Every step toward progress has been met by resistance, fueling an ongoing dance of advance and retreat; once crises subside, many institutions resort to the same exclusionary practices that resulted in settlements, social movements, and diversity initiatives to begin with.

Just as waves of epic change during Reconstruction and the Civil Rights Movement receded, any progress today must be viewed as ephemeral, not finite. Lasting change will require constant vigilance.

But it is also clear that every instance of progress has been advanced by courageous men and women who have defied the avalanche of reasons they have been given to succumb to inertia. They rose to the myriad challenges—the antiquated attitudes or inadequate pipelines—viewing them not as unalterable facts but as correctable consequences of history. As the protracted quest for diversity at Columbia University and Coca-Cola show, change does not come easily, nor is it possible to effect without the genuine will of those at the top. In those all-too-rare instances of progress, those leaders sought to inspire cooperative engagement rather than begrudging submission through bullying and shame.

Even the most courageous and moral leaders need support.

Quick fixes like unconscious bias training or climate surveys—no matter how expertly administered—cannot begin to address, let alone repair, the damage of centuries of demeaning images of racial, ethnic, and religious minorities still perpetuated in film, on television, in advertising, news outlets, on museum walls, public iconography, and, indeed, at every level of our educational system. Climate surveys predictably detect the symptoms, but not the cause, of bigoted ideology that takes root long before it flowers in the classroom or workplace. Change will require a major overhaul of our cultural ecology if we are to seriously uproot an ideology embedded in our curricula and in our mass media, museums, and public iconography that purport to express widely shared ideals.

Greater efforts must also be made to address a pervasive racial and cultural illiteracy and a perversion of history, which are unfortunate vestiges of America's global rise. They are pieces of a tragic legacy that we the people must neither forget nor reclaim if we are to realize *E pluribus unum.* But, this ambitious undertaking requires us to redefine—in a more expansive way—who We, as Americans, actually are.

Throughout its history, America has placed a premium on Whiteness as a barometer of elitism and identity. The multibillion-dollar diversity superstructure is built on this flawed foundation, its very existence a concession that a costly and redundant apparatus is required if racial equality is to be achieved. Even in instances of relative success, as in the case of Coca-Cola, the painstaking project suggests that diversity cannot take flight organically or without struggle. The undertaking might also advance the misperception that a Herculean effort is required to uplift a subordinate class. But we also know that inequality and injustice are created conditions embedded in an economic system that remains entrenched and impervious to change.

We know, too, that America's greatness, its magic, has always been its difference. Its wonder and magnificence defy metrics or methods. America is classical and jazz, country and reggae. It's

Marilyn Monroe and Dorothy Dandridge, Salma Hayek and Joan Chen. It's every conceivable color and cuisine and has been propelled forward by contributions to science, technology, culture, and aesthetics from people around the globe. While many of its non-White and male contributors remain unsung, no one race, ethnicity, nation, or gender can *honestly* claim the genius of human progress. This experiment called humanity is expansive and unimaginably deep and implicates us all. Only the uninformed and misinformed, the delusional or those with narcissistic impulses continue to cling to narratives of racial supremacy. Unfortunately, they have been ably assisted by an education and mass media establishment stubbornly bound to history.

In the end, racial diversity will not be ushered in by pledges, slogans, or well-compensated czars. While lawsuits will at times stymy progress or exact a price on the most egregious transgressors, racial diversity will only be achieved once White America is weaned off a prevailing narrative of racial preeminence—a belief system as intoxicating and addictive, and ultimately destructive, as any opiate. The seeds of this corrosive ideology are planted early, and a paradigm shift will require courageous leadership in every sphere, from elementary school principals to university presidents, and from parents, media, and art makers to corporate CEOs. Without Truth, there cannot be Justice, and the insidious vapor of bigotry will continue to pervade our monochromatic workplaces and our schools and infect public discourse too often laced with hate. Yes, change will require resources and resolve, but no amount of money, no degree of effort, will succeed alongside a willful negation of our shared humanity.

In the end, Americans will rise together or submit to division and defeat. Either way, a force greater than us all is hurling us into a future in which we'll arrive broken or intact, in conflict or in peace, battle-bruised or unblemished, limping or strutting— but Americans we'll all be, variously arrayed in our multicolored, many-splendored glory.

ACKNOWLEDGMENTS

I am deeply indebted to a number of individuals and institutions for their generous support throughout the research and writing of this book. I am enormously grateful for the sabbatical support provided by New York University and for residency fellowships at the MacDowell Artist Colony in Peterborough, New Hampshire, and Maison Dora Maar in Menerbes, France, courtesy of the Brown Foundation. I cannot imagine more gracious hospitality or idyllic settings to wrestle with challenging material. At both residencies I was inspired daily by my fellow fellows and at MacDowell was especially honored to be housed in the cottage once inhabited by James Baldwin and to be named an Anne Cox Chambers Fellow.

I am ever grateful to the numerous people who sometimes granted multiple interviews without which this book would not be possible. There are too many to thank here, but their anecdotes and insights animate these pages.

A special thanks to Cyrus Mehri for the many meetings and conversations, for the avalanche of articles and reports, and for generously helping me secure interviews with key sources. I'm also indebted to friends and colleagues for facilitating introductions to sources whose contributions proved invaluable. For this

I owe special thanks to Nevah Assang, Judy and Janell Byrd, John Coatsworth, Regina Hall, Lyle Ashton Harris, Crystal McCrary, and Deb Willis.

I extend a bouquet of thanks to Alessandra Bagli for her enthusiastic support from the start; my agent, Neeti Madan; Maia Hibbett for her research support; the amazing team at Hachette; and, last but far from least, Katy O'Donnell at Bold Type Books for her probing questions and wise and caring editorial guidance.

And finally, I'm eternally grateful to my amazing family—especially my husband, Michael; my sister, Dorothy; and my daughters, Marjani and Mykel—and my network of colleagues and friends for being a vital source of encouragement, humor, and light.

NOTES

PREFACE

1. "Race/Ethnicity of College Faculty," National Center for Education Statistics (NCES), accessed May 1, 2019, https://nces.ed.gov /fastfacts/display.asp?id=61. Among full-time professors in 2016, 55 percent were males; 27 percent were females; 7 percent were Asian/Pacific Islander males; and 2 percent each were Asian/Pacific Islander females, Black males, Hispanic males, and Black females. The following groups each made up 1 percent or less of the total number of full-time professors: Hispanic females, individuals of two or more races, and American Indian/ Alaska Native individuals.

2. NCES. Native Americans, who are less than 1 percent of the US population, make up less than 1 percent of professors.

3. NCES. This compares to Asians, who at roughly 6 percent of the US population hold 9 percent of full-time professors hips—roughly 40 percent of whom are foreign nationals.

4. "2017 Survey," American Society of News Editors, https://www .asne.org/diversity-survey-2017.

5. US Census Bureau, "American Indian and Alaska Native Heritage Month: November 2017," Census.gov, October 6, 2017, accessed May 1, 2019, https://www.census.gov/newsroom/facts-for-features/2017/aian-month.html.

CHAPTER 1: DIVERSITY AND DISCONTENT

1. "Report of the National Advisory Commission on Civil Disorders," 1968.

2. That compared to 90 percent of Asians and 62 percent of Hispanics.

3. Author interview, Clarence Otis, November 29, 2017.

4. Theresa Johnston, "Clarence Otis: Leading a Casual Dining Empire," *Stanford Lawyer* 88 (Spring 2013), accessed May 1, 2019, https://law.stanford.edu/stanford-lawyer/articles/clarence-otis-leading-a-casual-dining-.

5. Author interview, Clarence Otis, February 22, 2019.

6. "Missing Pieces Report: The 2016 Board Diversity Census of Women and Minorities on Fortune 500 Boards," *Catalyst*, January 16, 2019, accessed May 1, 2019, https://www.catalyst.org/research/missing-pieces-report-the-2018-board-diversity-census-of-women-and-minorities-on-fortune-500-boards/.

7. Grace Donnelly, "The Number of Black CEOs at Fortune 500 Companies Is at Its Lowest Since 2002," *Fortune*, February 28, 2019, accessed May 1, 2019, http://Fortune.com/2018/02/28/Black-History-Month-Black-Ceos-Fortune-500/.

8. See EEOC Report, 2016.

9. "Dr. King Is Felled by Rock," *Chicago Tribune*, August 6, 1966.

10. Carol Anderson, *White Rage: The Unspoken Truth of Our Racial Divide* (New York: Bloomsbury, 2016).

11. Author interview, Darren Walker, December 19, 2016.

12. Author interview, Darren Walker, December 19, 2016.

13. Roger Schonfeld, Mariet Westermann, and Liam Sweeney, "Art Museum Staff Demographic Survey," Andrew W. Mellon Foundation, July 28, 2014, 4.

14. Wilson's groundbreaking 1992 *Mining the Museum* exhibit at the Maryland Historical Society juxtaposed objects in the collection to highlight museum practices of exclusion and omission. Also see https://museumsandrace.org.

15. Katie Richards, "Burberry Apologizes for Sending Hoodie with Strings Resembling a Noose Down the Runway," *Adweek*, February 19, 2019.

16. "Fashion Has a Diversity Problem on the Business Side, Too," *The Business of Fashion*, May 2, 2018, https://www.businessoffashion.com

/articles/professional/fashion-has-a-diversity-problem-on-the-business
-side-too.

17. Liz Spayd, "Preaching the Gospel of Diversity, but Not Following It," *New York Times*, December 17, 2016, https://www.nytimes.com/2016 /12/17/public-editor/new-york-times-diversity-liz-spayd-public-editor .html?smid=tw-share.

18. He succeeded Jill Abramson, the first woman to hold that position at the *New York Times*.

19. See American Society of News Editors, "Newsroom Diversity Survey," https://www.asne.org/newsroom_diversitysurvey.

20. "Diversity and Inclusion Report," *New York Times*, 2018, https:// www.nytco.com/company/diversity-and-inclusion/2018-diversity-inclusion -report/.

21. "Diversity and Inclusion Report."

22. "2017 Survey," American Society of News Editors.

23. ASNE, "Table 0. Employees by Minority Group," ASNE 2017, https://www.asne.org/content.asp?contentid=147.

24. "NABJ Reacts to CBS Political Unit Hirings," National Association of Black Journalists, January 15, 2019, https://www.nabj.org/news /433871/NABJ-Reacts-to-CBS-Political-Unit-Hirings.htm.

25. John Horn, Nicole Sperling, and Doug Smith, "Oscar Voters Overwhelmingly White, Male," *Los Angeles Times*, February 19, 2012.

26. Ryan Faughnder, "Study Finds 'Inclusion Crisis' at Hollywood Studios," *Los Angeles Times*, February 22, 2016, https://www.latimes.com /entertainment/tv/la-et-ct-epidemic-of-invisibility-hollywood-20160222 -story.html.

27. "Digest of Education Statistics," National Center for Education Statistics, 2017, accessed June 1, 2019, https://nces.ed.gov/programs /digest/d17/tables/dt17_318.45.asp.

28. Blanca Myers, "Women and Minorities in Tech, by the Numbers," *Wired*, March 27, 2018, https://www.wired.com/story/computer-science -graduates-diversity/.

29. Daisuke Wakabayashi, "Google Fires Engineer Who Wrote Memo Questioning Women in Tech," *New York Times*, August 7, 2017,

https://www.nytimes.com/2017/08/07/business/google-women-engineer
-fired-memo.html.

30. Jessica Guynn, "Twitter Diversity Pick Stirs Controversy," *USA Today*, updated December 30, 2015, https://www.usatoday.com/story/tech /2015/12/29/twitter-diversity-chief-apple-white-man/78036978/.

31. Josh Dawsey, "Trump Derides Protection for Immigrants from 'Shithole' Countries," *Washington Post*, January 12, 2018, https://www.wash ingtonpost.com/politics/trump-attacks-protections-for-immigrants-from -shithole-countries-in-oval-office-meeting/2018/01/11/bfc0725c-f711 -11e7-91af-31ac729add94_story.html?utm_term=.80d88a5ad8f3.

32. Donald J. Trump, https://twitter.com/realdonaldtrump/status /1015033658548207616?lang=en.

33. NCES.

34. Don Gonyea, "Majority of White Americans Say They Believe Whites Face Discrimination," NPR, October 24, 2017, https://www.npr .org/2017/10/24/559604836/majority-of-white-americans-think-theyre -discriminated-against.

35. Stav Ziv, "Many Americans Have More in Common with White Nationalists Than They Think, Poll Finds," *Newsweek*, September 15, 2017.

36. Peyton M. Craighill and Sean Sullivan, "The Wide Racial Gap in Obama's Presidential Elections, in 2 Charts," *Washington Post*, August 28, 2013, https://www.washingtonpost.com/news/the-fix/wp/2013/08/28 /the-wide-racial-gap-in-obamas-presidential-elections-in-2-charts/?utm _term=.35d29069cfab.

37. Brian Thompson, "The Racial Wealth Gap: Addressing America's Most Pressing Epidemic," *Forbes*, February 18, 2018, https://www.forbes .com/sites/brianthompson1/2018/02/18/the-racial-wealth-gap-address ing-americas-most-pressing-epidemic/#6034460a7a48.

38. Tim Wise, "Is Sisterhood Conditional?: White Women and the Rollback of Affirmative Action," Tim Wise (blog), September 23, 1998, http://www.timwise.org/1998/09/is-sisterhood-conditional-white -women-and-the-rollback-of-affirmative-action/.

39. Frank Dobbin and Alexandra Kalev, "Why Diversity Programs Fail," *Harvard Business Review*, July–August 2016.

40. Christopher Ingraham, "The 'Smoking Gun' Proving North Carolina Republicans Tried to Disenfranchise Black Voters," *Washington Post*, July 29, 2016, https://www.washingtonpost.com/news/wonk/wp/2016 /07/29/the-smoking-gun-proving-north-carolina-republicans-tried-to -disenfranchise-black-voters/?utm_term=.796ad99b93f6.

41. David Leonhardt, "Our Broken Economy, in One Simple Chart," *New York Times*, August 7, 2017, https://www.nytimes.com/interactive /2017/08/07/opinion/leonhardt-income-inequality.html.

42. "ADP National Employment Report: Private Sector Employment Increased by 177,000 Jobs in June," ADP, July 5, 2018, https://www .adpemploymentreport.com/2018/June/NER/docs/ADP-NATIONAL -EMPLOYMENT-REPORT-June2018-Final-Press-Release.pdf.

43. International Labor Organization, "Greening with Jobs: World Employment and Social Outlook 2008," ILO, https://www.ilo.org/weso -greening/#Intro-2; Marshall Burke, W. Matthew Davis, and Noah Diffenbaugh, "Large Potential Reduction in Economic Damages under UN Mitigation Targets," *Nature*, May 23, 2018, 549–553.

CHAPTER 2: THROUGH THE LOOKING GLASS

1. "Rastus' Riotous Ride," IMDbPro, accessed June 1, 2019, https:// pro.imdb.com/title/tt0135622?s=bab58a50-f63e-23bd-1638-81b4734 fa63b.

2. Letter to Darr Smith, August 2, 1949, Letter in Fredi Washington Papers [microform], 1922–1981, Schomburg Center for Research in Black Culture.

3. Fredi Washington Papers, Schomburg Center for Research for Black Culture, NYPL, included in LFBA.

4. Letter to Darr Smith, August 2, 1949, Letter in Fredi Washington Papers [microform], 1922–1981, Schomburg Center for Research in Black Culture.

5. Michael Quintanilla, "Raquel's Beauty: She Shows Her Roots," *Los Angeles Times*, June 14, 2001, https://www.latimes.com/archives/la -xpm-2001-jun-14-cl-10226-story.html.

6. Pamela Newkirk, "Fredi Washington's Forgotten War on Hollywood," in *Women and Migration: Responses in Art and History*, ed. Deborah Willis, Ellyn Toscano, and Kalia Brooks Nelson (Cambridge, UK: Open Book Publishers, 2019), https://doi.org/10.11647/obp.0153.

7. Langston Hughes and Milton Meltzer, *Black Magic: A Pictorial History of Black Entertainers in America* (New York: Bonanza Books, 1967), 288–289.

8. Hughes and Meltzer, *Black Magic*, 293.

9. Hughes and Meltzer, *Black Magic*, 294.

10. Berry in conversation with *Teen Vogue* editor Elaine Weleroth at the Cannes Lions International Festival of Creativity.

11. Alice George, "Was the 1968 TV Show 'Julia' a Milestone or a Millstone for Diversity," Smithsonian.com, September 6, 2018, https://www.smithsonianmag.com/smithsonian-institution/was-1968-tv-show-julia-milestone-or-millstone-180970198/.

12. Author interview, Susan Fales-Hill, November 15, 2018.

13. Author interview, Tim Reid, November 16, 2018.

14. Matthew Sweet, "Snakes, Slaves and Seduction," *Guardian*, February 6, 2008. Also see Edward Sakamoto, "Anna May Wong and the Dragon-Lady Syndrome," *Los Angeles Times*, July 12, 1987.

15. *Life Magazine*, March 1, 1954.

16. Author interview, Alex Nogales, December 18, 2018.

17. Author interview, Alex Nogales, December 18, 2018.

18. Lincoln, "Latino Group NHLA Joins Call for Greater Diversity at Paramount."

19. Author interview, Alex Nogales, December 18, 2018.

20. Smith et al., "Inclusion or Invisibility," 16.

21. Stacy L. Smith, Marc Choueiti, and Katherine Pieper, "Inequality in 900 Popular Films: Examining Portrayals of Gender, Race/Ethnicity, LGBT, and Disability from 2007 to 2016," Institute for Diversity and Empowerment at Annenberg (IDEA), USC Annenberg School for Communication and Journalism, 24, https://annenberg.usc.edu/sites/default/files/Dr_Stacy_L_Smith-Inequality_in_900_Popular_Films.pdf.

22. Smith et al., "Inequality in 900 Popular Films," 22.

23. Stacy L. Smith et al., "Inclusion in the Director's Chair: Gender, Race, & Age of Directors Across 1,200 Top Films from 2007 to 2018," USC Annenberg Inclusion Initiative, January 2019, 3.

24. Author interview, Gina Prince-Bythewood, November 20, 2018.

25. Author interview, Gina Prince-Bythewood, November 20, 2018.

26. Author interview, Gina Prince-Bythewood, November 20, 2018.

27. Author interview, George Tillman, November 23, 2018.

28. Author interview, George Tillman, November 23, 2018.

29. Darnell Hunt et al., "Hollywood Diversity Report 2018: Five Years of Progress and Missed Opportunities," UCLA College of Social Sciences, February 2018, https://socialsciences.ucla.edu/wp-content/uploads/2018 /02/UCLA-Hollywood-Diversity-Report-2018-2-27-18.pdf.

30. Hunt et al., "Hollywood Diversity Report 2018."

31. Hunt et al., "Hollywood Diversity Report 2018."

32. Lily Rothman, "The Best Man Holiday Is Not Like Other Blockbusters—But Not Because of Race," *Time*, November 19, 2013.

33. Author interview, Misan Sagay, December 2, 2018.

34. Linda Holmes, "'The Best Man Holiday' and the Language of Expectations," NPR, November 18, 2013, https://www.npr.org/2013/11 /18/245941099/the-best-man-holiday-and-the-language-of-expectations.

35. Author interview, Malcolm Lee, October 26, 2018.

36. Author interview, Malcolm Lee, October 26, 2018.

37. Scott Mendelson, "Review: 'The Hate U Give' Is an Oscar-Worthy Masterpiece," *Forbes*, October 1, 2018, https://www.forbes.com/sites /scottmendelson/2018/10/01/review-the-hate-u-give-is-an-oscar-worthy -masterpiece/#77015e5a1627; Owen Gleiberman, "'The Hate U Give': A Racial Drama So Honest Every American Should See It," *Variety*, October 21, 2018, https://variety.com/2018/film/columns/the-hate-u-give -amandla-stenberg-1202987675/.

38. While *Do the Right Thing* was not nominated for Best Picture, it was nominated for Original Screenplay, and Danny Aiello was nominated for Best Supporting Actor.

39. Author interview, George Tillman Jr.

40. Holmes, "'The Best Man Holiday' and the Language of Expectations."

41. Hilary Lewis, "Oscars: Spike Lee Refuses to Attend Awards Due to All-White Acting Nominees," *Hollywood Reporter*, January 18, 2016, https://www.hollywoodreporter.com/news/spike-lee-wont-attend-oscars-856676.

42. Stephen Galloway, "Academy President Issues Lengthy Statement on Lack of Oscars Diversity," *Hollywood Reporter*, January 18, 2016, https://www.hollywoodreporter.com/news/oscars-academy-president-cheryl-boone-857016.

43. Michael Schulman, "Shakeup at the Oscars," *The New Yorker*, February 27, 2017.

44. Galloway, "Academy President Issues Lengthy Statement."

45. Schulman, "Shakeup at the Oscars."

46. Author interview, April Reign, January 11, 2019.

47. Joanna Robinson, "Green Book Wins Best Picture; Spike Lee and Twitter Get Out Their Knives," *Vanity Fair*, February 25, 2019.

48. Author interview, E. Brian Dobbins, November 5, 2018.

49. Author interview, Misan Sagay, December 2, 2018.

50. Marc Choueiti, Stacy L. Smith, and Katherine Pieper, "Critic's Choice: Gender and Race/Ethnicity of Film Reviewers," USC Annenberg Inclusion Initiative, June 2018, 10.

51. Daniel Arkin, "Brie Larson Calls for More Diversity in Film Criticism Following USC Study," nbcnews.com, June 14, 2018, https://www.nbcnews.com/pop-culture/movies/brie-larson-calls-more-diversity-film-criticism-following-usc-study-n883141.

52. Arkin, "Brie Larson Calls for More Diversity in Film Criticism."

53. Choueiti, Smith, and Pieper, "Critic's Choice," 10.

54. Smith et al., "Inclusion in the Director's Chair," 19.

55. Author interview, Misan Sagay, December 2, 2018.

56. Author interview, George Tillman, November 23, 2018.

CHAPTER 3: RAGING TOWERS

1. Isaac Stanley Becker, "A Confrontation over Race at Yale: Hundreds of Students Demand Answers from the School's First Black Dean," *Washington Post*, November 5, 2015.

2. Becker, "A Confrontation over Race at Yale."

3. Anemona Hartocollis, "Yale Lecturer Resigns after Email on Halloween Costumes," *New York Times*, December 7, 2015.

4. Hartocollis, "Yale Lecturer Resigns after Email on Halloween Costumes."

5. Isaac Stanley-Becker, "Yale's President Tells Minority Students: 'We Failed You,'" *Washington Post*, November 6, 2015.

6. Jonathan Holloway, "Letter from Yale College Dean Jonathan Holloway," November 9, 2019, Yale, https://faculty.yale.edu/news /president-and-yale-college-dean-underscore-commitment-better-yale.

7. Elahe Izadi, "Harvard Law Has 'Serious' Racism Problem, Dean Says after Black Professors' Portraits Defaced," *Washington Post*, November 19, 2015, https://www.washingtonpost.com/news/grade-point/wp /2015/11/19/defacing-of-black-harvard-professor-portraits-investigated -as-hate-crime/?utm_term=.6df94ec8133c.

8. Susan Svrluga, "U. Missouri President, Chancellor Resign over Handling of Racial Incidents," *Washington Post*, November 9, 2015, https://www.washingtonpost.com/news/grade-point/wp/2015/11/09 /missouris-student-government-calls-for-university-presidents-removal/ ?utm_term=.9aa1df39efef.

9. Leslie Houts Picca and Joe R. Feagin, *Two Faced Racism: Whites in the Backstage and Frontstage* (London: Routledge, 2007).

10. While the governor initially apologized for appearing in a yearbook photograph in blackface, he later said it wasn't him, and an investigation failed to confirm the identity of the two students.

11. Jon Cohen, "Zimmerman Verdict: 86 Percent of African Americans Disapprove," *Washington Post*, July 22, 2013, https://www.washingtonpost .com/news/post-politics/wp/2013/07/22/zimmerman-verdict-86-percent -of-african-americans-disapprove/?utm_term=.cdcc3a33e9d3.

12. "Sharp Racial Divisions in Reaction to Brown, Garner Decisions," Pew Resarch Center Poll, December 8, 2018, https://www.people-press .org/2014/12/08/sharp-racial-divisions-in-reactions-to-brown-garner -decisions/.

13. Nazgol Ghandnoosh, "Race and Punishment: Racial Perceptions of Crime and Support for Punitive Policies," Sentencing Project,

September 3, 2014, https://www.sentencingproject.org/publications/race
-and-punishment-racial-perceptions-of-crime-and-support-for-punitive
-policies/.

14. Dan Gramlich, "From Police to Parole, Black and White Americans Differ Widely in Their Views of Criminal Justice System," Pew
Research Organization, May 21, 2019, accessed June 2, 2019, https://www
.pewresearch.org/fact-tank/2019/05/21/from-police-to-parole-black
-and-white-americans-differ-widely-in-their-views-of-criminal-justice
-system/.

15. "In Maryland, Black People Found to Be 3 Times More Likely to
Be Arrested for Marijuana Possession Than White People, Despite Equal
Usage Rates," ACLU, June 4, 2013, https://www.aclu.org/press-releases
/maryland-black-people-found-be-3-times-more-likely-be-arrested
-marijuana-possession.

16. Author interview, Michael Middleton, October 8, 2018.

17. Britton O'Daly, "Yale Responds after Black Student Reported
for Napping in Common Room," *Yale News*, May 10, 2018, https://
yaledailynews.com/blog/2018/05/10/yale-responds-after-black-student
-reported-for-napping-in-common-room/.

18. Heather Mac Donald, "Rage and Race at Yale," *National Review*,
May 24, 2018, https://www.nationalreview.com/magazine/2018/06/11
/yale-racial-grievances-university-bows-diversity-enforcers/.

19. Conor Friedersdorf, "A Dialogue on Race and Speech at Yale," *The
Atlantic*, March 24, 2016, https://www.theatlantic.com/politics/archive
/2016/03/yale-silliman-race/475152/.

20. Ashley Jardina, Sean McElwee, and Spencer Piston, "How Do
Trump Supporters See Black People?" *Slate*, November 7, 2016, https://
slate.com/news-and-politics/2016/11/the-majority-of-trump-supporters
-surveyed-described-black-people-as-less-evolved.html.

21. Rebecca C. Hetey and Jennifer L. Eberhardt, "Racial Disparities
in Incarceration Increase Acceptance of Punitive Policies," *Psychological Science* 25, no. 10 (2014), 1949–1954, https://web.stanford.edu/class
/comm1a/readings/hetey-disparities.pdf.

22. Jennifer L. Eberhardt et al., "Looking Deathworthy: Perceived
Stereotypicality of Black Defendants Predicts Capital-Sentencing

Outcomes," *Psychological Science* 17, no. 5 (May 2006): 41, http://scholarship.law.cornell.edu/lsrp_papers/41.

23. Thomas Jesse Jones, "Negro Education: A Study of the Private and Higher Schools for Colored People in the United States," Bulletin, Bureau of Education, 1916, vol. 2, no. 39, 22.

24. Jones, "Negro Education."

25. Jones, "Negro Education," 23.

26. Pamela Newkirk, "Tuskegee's Talented Tenth: Reconciling a Legacy," *Journal of Asian and African Studies* 51, no. 3 (2016), https://doi.org/10.1177%2F0021909615612113.

27. Edna Chun and Alvin Evans, *Leading a Diversity Culture Shift in Higher Education* (New York: Routledge, 2018), 8.

28. Martin J. Finkelstein, Valerie Martin Conley, and Jack H. Schuster, "Taking the Measure of Faculty Diversity," TIAA Institute, April 2016, https://www.tiaainstitute.org/publication/taking-measure-faculty-diversity.

29. Chun and Evans, *Leading a Diversity Culture Shift in Higher Education*, 221.

30. Author interview, Richard Bribiescas, October 17, 2018.

31. Author interview, Richard Bribiescas, October 17, 2018.

CHAPTER 4: CIVIL WARS: LEGACY OF AN INGLORIOUS PAST

1. Daniel G. Brinton, "The Aims of Anthropology," *Popular Science Monthly* 48, no. 1 (November 1895): 69, https://en.wikisource.org/wiki/Popular_Science_Monthly/Volume_48/November_1895/The_Aims_of_Anthropology.

2. Lee D. Baker, "Daniel G. Brinton's Success on the Road to Obscurity, 1890–99," *Cultural Anthropology* 3, no. 15 (2000): 394–423.

3. One of Princeton's cofounders was Rev. Ebenezer Pemberton, Osborn's ancestor, whose family had made their fortune in the slave trade and from the sale of rum, sugar, tobacco, and rice produced by enslaved Africans in the West Indies. After earning his undergraduate and Doctor of Science, Osborn became a lecturer and then professor of comparative anatomy and later went to Columbia, where he eventually became the first

dean of pure science. He would go on to become a fellow of the American Academy of Arts and Sciences, receive honorary doctorates from Oxford and Cambridge, and achieve fame for naming the *Tyrannosaurus rex*. For nearly twenty-five years, beginning in 1908, he would serve as director of the American Museum of Natural History.

4. Madison Grant, *The Passing of the Great Race, or The Racial Basis of European History*, 4th rev. ed. (New York: Charles Scribner & Sons), 1936, https://archive.org/stream/passingofgreatra00granuoft/passingofgreatra 00granuoft_djvu.txt.

5. Jonathan Spiro, *Defending the Master Race: Conservation, Eugenics and the Legacy of Madison Grant* (Lebanon, NH: University Press of New England, 2009), 158.

6. Charles Murray and Richard Hernstein, *The Bell Curve: Intelligence and Class Structure in American Life* (New York: Free Press, 1994).

7. Craig Steven Wilder, *Ebony and Ivy: Race, Slavery, and the Troubled History of America's Universities* (New York: Bloomsbury Press, 2014), 182.

8. Wilder, *Ebony and Ivy*, 67.

9. Wilder, *Ebony and Ivy*, 71.

10. Wilder, *Ebony and Ivy*, 105.

11. Wilder, *Ebony and Ivy*, 114.

12. Wilder, *Ebony and Ivy*, 10.

13. Wilder, *Ebony and Ivy*, 11.

14. Author interview, Kirt von Daacke, December 20, 2018.

15. Author interview, Cecelia Moore, November 16, 2018.

16. Adeel Hassan, "3 Confederate Statues Will Remain at North Carolina Capitol," *New York Times*, August 22, 2018.

17. Author interview, Cecelia Moore, November 16, 2018.

18. Author interview, Kirt von Daacke, December 20, 2018.

19. Susan Svrluga, "The Harvard Law Shield Tied to Slavery Is Already Disappearing, after Corporation Vote," *Washington Post*, March 15, 2016, https://www.washingtonpost.com/news/grade-point/wp/2016 /03/15/the-harvard-law-shield-tied-to-slavery-is-already-disappearing -after-corporation-vote/.

20. "Library Exhibit Looks at the History of the Former Harvard Law School Shield," *Harvard Law Today*, September 16, 2016, https://

today.law.harvard.edu/library-exhibit-looks-history-former-harvard-law -school-shield/.

21. Max Kutner, "Princeton Is Keeping Woodrow Wilson's Name Despite Student Protests," *Newsweek*, April 4, 2016, https://www.news week.com/princeton-woodrow-wilson-name-protests-443858.

22. "Report of the Trustee Ad Hoc Committee on Diversity," Princeton University, September 8–10, 2013, accessed March 30, 2019, https:// inclusive.princeton.edu/sites/inclusive/files/pu-report-on-diversity.pdf.

23. Will Dudley, "A Message Regarding the Violence in Charlottesville," Washington and Lee University, August 14, 2017, https://www.wlu .edu/presidents-office/messages-to-the-community/a-message-regarding -the-violence-in-charlottesville.

24. "Report of the Commission on Institutional History and Community," Washington and Lee University, 2018, https://www.wlu.edu /presidents-office/issues-and-initiatives/commission-on-institutional-history -and-community/report-of-the-commission-on-institutional-history-and -community/part-iii-physical-campus.

25. "Report of the Commission on Institutional History and Community," Washington and Lee University.

26. T. Rees Shapiro, "Washington and Lee University to Remove Confederate Flags Following Protests," *Washington Post*, July 8, 2014, https://www.washingtonpost.com/local/education/washington-and-lee -university-to-remove-confederate-flags-following-protests/2014/07/08 /e219e580-06bb-11e4-8a6a-19355c7e870a_story.html.

27. "Report of the Brown University Steering Committee on Slavery and Justice," Brown University, October 2006, 1, http://brown.edu /Research/Slavery_Justice/#.

28. Author interview, Kirt Von Daacke, December 20, 2018.

CHAPTER 5: COURSE CORRECTION

1. Author interview, Dennis Mitchell, April 26, 2018.

2. Adam Harris, "The Supreme Court Justice Who Forever Changed Affirmative Action," *The Atlantic*, October 13, 2018, https:// www.theatlantic.com/education/archive/2018/10/how-lewis-powell -changed-affirmative-action/572938/.

3. Anthony Lewis, "'Bakke' May Change a Lot While Changing No Law," *New York Times*, July 2, 1978, https://www.nytimes.com/1978/07/02/archives/bakke-may-change-a-lot-while-changing-no-law.html.

4. Lincoln Caplan, "Thurgood Marshall and the Need for Affirmative Action," *The New Yorker*, December 9, 2015, https://www.newyorker.com/news/news-desk/thurgood-marshall-and-the-need-for-affirmative-action.

5. Author interview, Lee Bollinger, October 24, 2018.

6. Lyle Denniston, "Opinion Recap: More Rigorous Race Review," SCOTUSblog, June 24, 2013, http://www.scotusblog.com/2013/06/opinion-recap-more-rigorous-race-review/.

7. Author interview, Lee Bollinger, October 24, 2018.

8. Author interview, Lee Bollinger, October 24, 2018.

9. "Policy and Planning Equity Reports," Columbia University, Faculty of Arts and Science, October 2018, https://fas.columbia.edu/files/fas/content/Columbia-ArtsandSciences-PPC-Equity-Reports-2018.pdf.

10. Author interview, Dennis Mitchell, April 26, 2018.

11. "Policy and Planning Committee Equity Reports," Columbia University, October 2018.

12. Karen Xia and Noah Percy, "Columbia Has $185 Million in Dedicated Funds. Why Is Hiring Diverse Faculty Still So Difficult?" *Columbia Spectator*, February 1, 2019, https://www.columbiaspectator.com/news/2019/02/01/columbia-has-185-million-in-dedicated-funds-why-is-hiring-diverse-faculty-still-so-difficult-9/.

13. "ACEJMC Accrediting Standards," Accrediting Council on Education in Journalism and Mass Communications, accessed May 2, 2018, http://acejmc.ku.edu/PROGRAM/STANDARDS.SHTML.

14. "ACEJMC Accrediting Standards," Accrediting Council on Education in Journalism and Mass Communications.

15. "Diversity Tip Sheet," Accrediting Council on Education in Journalism and Mass Communications, accessed May 2, 2018, http://www.acejmc.org/wp-content/uploads/2017/08/Diversity-Tipsheet.pdf.

16. "Diversity Tip Sheet," Accrediting Council on Education in Journalism and Mass Communications.

17. Author interview, Dennis Mitchell, April 26, 2018.

18. Author interview, Edna Chun, October 2, 2018

19. Lauren Rivera, *Pedigree: How Elite Students Get Elite Jobs* (Princeton, NJ: Princeton University Press, 2016), 9.

20. Helen Zia, *Asian American Dreams: The Emergence of an American People* (New York: Farrar, Straus and Giroux, 2000), 28.

21. Rakesh Kochhar and Anthony Cilluffo, "Key Findings on the Rise in Income Inequality within America's Racial and Ethnic Groups," Pew Research Center, FactTank, July 12, 2018, http://www.pewresearch.org/fact-tank/2018/07/12/key-findings-on-the-rise-in-income-inequality-within-americas-racial-and-ethnic-groups/.

22. Michael Hurwitz, "The Impact of Legacy Status on Undergraduate Admissions at Elite Colleges and Universities," Harvard Graduate School of Education, December 2009, https://scholar.harvard.edu/files/btl/files/michael_hurwitz_-_qp_12-12-09.pdf.

23. Jessica M. Wang and Brian P. Yu, "Makeup of the Class," *Harvard Crimson Review*, accessed May 21, 2019, https://features.thecrimson.com/2017/freshman-survey/makeup/.

24. Rivera, *Pedigree*, 4.

25. "New Study Shows Asian American Support for Affirmative Action," NBC News, October 6, 2014, https://www.nbcnews.com/news/asian-america/new-study-shows-asian-american-support-affirmative-action-n213976.

26. Author interview, Lee Bollinger, October 24, 2018.

CHAPTER 6: CORPORATE AMERICA'S JOURNEY TO JUSTICE

1. Constance L. Hays, *The Real Thing: Truth and Power at the Coca-Cola Company* (New York: Random House, 2004), 205–206.

2. Author interview, Cyrus Mehri, October 25, 2018.

3. Hays, *The Real Thing*, 207.

4. Author interview, Bari-Ellen Roberts, January 9, 2019.

5. Bari-Ellen Roberts, *Roberts v. Texaco: A True Story of Race and Corporate America* (New York: Avon Books, 1998), 147.

6. Author interview, Cyrus Mehri, October 25, 2018.

7. Author interview, Cyrus Mehri, October 25, 2018.

8. Kurt Eichenwald, "Texaco Executives, on Tape, Discussed Imped-ing a Bias Suit," *New York Times*, November 4, 1996.

9. Eichenwald, "Texaco Executives, on Tape."

10. Mike France and Tim Smart, "The Ugly Talk on the Texaco Tape," *Bloomberg*, November 18, 1996.

11. Author interview, George Eddings Jr., January 16, 2019.

12. Hays, *The Real Thing*, 257.

13. "Coca-Cola Creates Diversity Council," *Jet*, June 14, 1999, 6.

14. Hays, *The Real Thing*, 301.

15. Henry Unger, "Exec in Coke Management Flap Promoted, Will Stay," *Atlanta Constitution*, January 5, 2000, 1A.

16. Henry Unger, "Coke Aims $1 Billion at Diversity; Program Focuses on Entrepreneurship for Women, Minorities in Local Communi-ties," *Atlanta Journal and Constitution*, May 16, 2000, 1A.

17. Russell Grantham, *Atlanta Journal and Constitution*, March 31, 2000, 4F.

18. Constance L. Hays, "Group of Black Employees Calls for Boycott of Coca-Cola Products," *New York Times*, April 20, 2000, C1.

19. Henry Unger and Maria Saporta, "Jesse Jackson Urges Coca-Cola to Settle," *Cox News Service*, April 19, 2000.

20. Unger and Saporta, "Jesse Jackson Urges Coca-Cola to Settle."

21. Alexis Herman et al., "First Annual Report of the Task Force," US District Court, Northern District of Georgia, 2002, https://www.coca-colacompany.com/content/dam/journey/us/en/private/fileassets/pdf/unknown/unknown/task_force_report.pdf.

22. Author interview, George Eddings Jr., January 16, 2019.

23. Alexis Herman et al., "First Annual Report of the Task Force."

24. Alexis Herman et al., "First Annual Report of the Task Force."

25. Author interview, Steve Bucherati, February 5, 2019.

26. Alexis Herman et al., "Second Annual Report of the Task Force," US District Court, Northern District of Georgia, December 1, 2003, https://www.coca-colacompany.com/content/dam/journey/us/en/private/fileassets/pdf/unknown/unknown/task_force_report_2003.pdf.

27. Author interview, Steve Bucherati, February 5, 2019.

28. Alexis M. Herman et al., "Fourth Annual Report of the Task Force," US District Court, Northern District of Georgia, December 1, 2006, https://www.coca-colacompany.com/content/dam/journey/us/en/private/fileassets/pdf/unknown/unknown/task_force_report_2005.pdf.

29. Herman et al., "Fourth Annual Report of the Task Force."

30. Alexis M. Herman et al., "Fifth Annual Report of the Task Force," US District Court, Northern District of Georgia, December 1, 2006, https://www.coca-colacompany.com/content/dam/journey/us/en/private/fileassets/pdf/unknown/unknown/task_force_report_2006.pdf.

31. Author interview, Steven Bucherati, February 5, 2019.

32. Caroline Wilbert, "Coke Praises Diversity Progress," *Atlanta Journal and Constitution*, October 29, 2005, G3.

33. Author interview, Ann Moore, February 7, 2019.

CHAPTER 7: ROONEY'S RULE

1. Author interview, Cyrus Mehri, October 25, 2018.

2. Johnnie L. Cochran Jr. and Cyrus Mehri, "Black Coaches in the National Football League: Superior Performance, Inferior Opportunities," Mehri & Skalet, PLLC, September 30, 2002.

3. Cochran and Mehri, "Black Coaches in the National Football League."

4. Author interview, Jeff Pash, January 7, 2019.

5. Author interview, Jeff Pash, January 7, 2019.

6. Author interview, Jeff Pash, January 7, 2019.

7. Author interview, Jeff Pash, January 7, 2019.

8. Leonard Shapiro, "Upshaw Says He's Opposed to Mehri-Cochran Plan," *Washington Post*, October 30, 2002, D2.

9. Leonard Shaprio, "Rooney Decries Tying Draft Picks to Hirings," *Washington Post*, November 11, 2002, D3.

10. Shaprio, "Rooney Decries Tying Draft Picks to Hirings."

11. Author interview, Jeff Pash, January 7, 2019.

12. Leonard Shapiro and Ken Denlinger, "Ravens Name Newsome NFL's First Black GM," *Washington Post*, November 26, 2002, https://www.washingtonpost.com/archive/sports/2002/11/26/ravens-name-newsome

-nfls-first-black-gm/15d8013d-3170-4e4a-a286-047e7f64c173/?utm
_term=.68de69828e91.

13. Author interview, Cyrus Mehri, October 25, 2018.

14. Polina Marinova and Grace Donnelly, "Inside Uber's Second Annual Diversity Report," *Fortune*, April 24, 2018, http://fortune.com /2018/04/24/uber-diversity-report-2/.

15. Author interview, Cyrus Mehri, October 25, 2018.

16. Mark Maske, "Lions' Millen Is Fined $200,000," *Washington Post*, July 26, 2003.

17. Jason Reid, "It's Time for the NFL to Take the Rooney Rule Seriously or Get Rid of It," *Washington Post*, January 2, 2018, https://www .washingtonpost.com/archive/sports/2002/11/26/ravens-name-newsome -nfls-first-black-gm/15d8013d-3170-4e4a-a286-047e7f64c173/?utm _term=.68de69828e91.

18. Mark Maske, "NFL Finds Raiders Complied with Rooney Rule after Investigation," *Washington Post*, January 19, 2018, ttps://www.wash ingtonpost.com/archive/sports/2002/11/26/ravens-name-newsome-nfls -first-black-gm/15d8013d-3170-4e4a-a286-047e7f64c173/?utm_term =.68de69828e91.

19. Author interview, Jeff Pash, January 7, 2019.

20. Author interview, Cyrus Mehri, January 3, 2019.

21. Author interview, Jeff Pash, January 7, 2019.

22. Author interview, Jeremi Duru, January 4, 2019.

23. Author interview, Jeff Pash, January 7, 2019.

24. Author interview, Jeremi Duru, January 4, 2019.

25. Author interview, Jeremi Duru, January 4, 2019.

26. Author interview, Jeff Pash, January 7, 2019.

27. Author interview, Cyrus Mehri, January 3, 2019.

CHAPTER 8: TURMOIL IN THE TRENCHES

1. Author interview, Tanya Odom, October 10, 2018.

2. Frank Dobbin and Alexandra Kalev, "Why Diversity Programs Fail," *Harvard Business Review*, July–August 2016, https://hbr.org/2016 /07/why-diversity-programs-fail.

3. "Fired Author of Controversial Google Memo Breaks His Silence," *CBS This Morning*, August 10, 2017, https://cbsnews.com/news /google-controversial-diversity-memo-james-damore-breaks0silence/.

4. Dobbin and Kalev, "Why Diversity Programs Fail."

5. Rohini Anand and Mary-Frances Winters, "A Retrospective View of Corporate Diversity Training from 1964 to the Present," *Academy of Management Learning & Education* 7, no. 3 (2008): 356–372.

6. Elizabeth Levy Paluck and Donald P. Green, "Prejudice Reduction: What Works: A Review and Assessment of Research and Practice," *Annual Review of Psychology* 60, no. 1 (2008): 339–367.

7. Paluck and Green, "Prejudice Reduction," 146.

8. Chun and Evans, *Leading a Diversity Culture Shift in Higher Education*, 146–147.

9. Chun and Evans, *Leading a Diversity Culture Shift in Higher Education*, 146–147.

10. Anand and Winters, "A Retrospective View of Corporate Diversity Training."

11. William B. Johnston et al., "Workforce 2000: Work and Workers for the 21st Century," Hudson Institute, Indianapolis, IN, June 1987.

12. Anand and Winters, "A Retrospective View of Corporate Diversity Training."

13. Matthew Penzarino, "Apple Diversity Head Denise Young Smith Apologizes for Controversial Choice of Words at Summit," TechCrunch, October 13, 2017, https://techcrunch.com/2017/10/13/apple-diversity -head-denise-young-smith-apologizes-for-controversial-choice-of -words-at-summit/.

14. Douglas Ernst, "Apple Executive Sorry for Saying White People Can Bring Diversity: 'I Regret the Choice of Words," *Washington Times*, October 16, 2017, https://www.washingtontimes.com/news/2017/oct/16 /apple-executive-sorry-for-saying-white-people-can-/.

15. Author interview, Steven Bucherati, February 5, 2019.

16. Dobbin and Kalven, "Why Diversity Programs Fail."

17. Paluck and Green, "Prejudice Reduction," 339–367.

18. L. Roberson, C. T. Kulik, and M. B. Pepper, "Individual and Environmental Factors Influencing the Use of Transfer Strategies after

Diversity Training," Group and Organization Management 34, no. 1 (2009): 67–89, https://doi.org/10.1177/1059601108329732.

19. Author interview, Tanya Odom, October 10, 2018.

20. Author interview, Tanya Odom, October 10, 2018.

21. Author interview, Richard Bribiescas, October 17, 2018.

22. Author interview, Edna Chun, December 7, 2018.

23. Author interview, Edna Chun, December 7, 2018.

24. Chun and Evans, *Leading a Diversity Culture Shift in Higher Education*, 50.

25. Author interview, Richard Bribiescas, October 17, 2018.

26. Stephanie K. Johnson and David R. Hekman, "Women and Minorities Are Penalized for Promoting Diversity," *Harvard Business Review*, March 23, 2016, https://hbr.org/2016/03/women-and-minorities -are-penalized-for-promoting-diversity.

27. Author interview, Edna Chun, December 7, 2018.

28. "Lawmaker's Bill Would Defund UT Office; Faculty Senate Preps for Meeting in Support of Chancellor," *Arizona Central*, December 7, 2015, https://www.azcentral.com/story/news/local/downtown-ut /2015/12/07/ut-faculty-senate-hold-emergency-meeting-amid-calls -chancellors-resignation/76917246/.

29. "Lawmaker's Bill Would Defund UT Office."

30. Susan Svriuga, "Republicans Threaten Funding Cuts after University Urges Leaving Christmas out of Holiday Celebrations," *Washington Post*, December 8, 2015.

31. Svriuga, "Republicans Threaten Funding Cuts."

32. Taylor Telford, "White Christian Conservative Males Will Suffer If School Hires Diversity Director, Lawmaker Says," *Washington Post*, August 23, 2018, https://www.washingtonpost.com/education /2018/08/23/state-senator-worried-about-white-christian-conservative -males-amid-nebraska-search-diversity-director/?utm_term=.0af0a 805219f.

33. Author interview, Edna Chun, December 7, 2018.

34. Author interview, Cyrus Merhi, December 21, 2018.

35. Author interview, Cyrus Mehri and Pamela Coukos, December 21, 2018.

36. Author interview, Michael Middleton, October 8, 2018.

CHAPTER 9: DIVERSITY, INC.

1. Stephanie Armour, "Debate Revived on Workplace Diversity," *USA Today*, July 21, 2003; F. Hansen, "Diversity's Business Case: Doesn't Add Up," *Workforce* 82, no. 4 (2003): 28–32.

2. Tina Shah Paikeday, Harsonal Sachar, Alix Stuart, and Cissy Young, "A Leader's Guide: Finding and Keeping Your Next Diversity Officer," Russell Reynolds Associates, 2019, https://www.russellreynolds .com/en/Insights/thoughtleadership/Documents/A%20Leaders%20Guide %20to%20Finding%20and%20Keeping%20Your%20Next%20Chief %20Diversity%20Officer.pdf.

3. According to figures cited on Tufts's website, last accessed April 2, 2019, https://ase.tufts.edu/faculty/diversity/.

4. Based on figures on Cornell's website, last accessed April 2, 2019, http://irp.dpb.cornell.edu/university-factbook/diversity.

5. "Welcome," Diversity First Certification Program, accessed June 2019, http://diversitycertificationprogram.org/about/welcome/.

6. Peter Schmidt, "'Black Issues in Higher Education' to Change Its Name to Reflect New Focus on Diverse Issues," *Chronicle of Higher Education*, July 22, 2005.

7. Author interview, Clarence Otis, January 21, 2019.

8. "Diversity at a Glance: The Data," digital image, Leadership Council on Legal Diversity, https://www.lcldnet.org/media/uploads/resource/Diver sity_at_a_Glance_V1.png.

9. "2016 Job Patterns for Minorities and Women in Private Industry (EEO-1)," US Equal Employment Opportunity Commission, accessed April 2, 2019, https://www1.eeoc.gov/eeoc/statistics/employment/jobpat -eeo1/2016/index.cfm.

10. David Cohen, "Women, Minorities Are Still Underrepresented on the Boards of Social Media and Tech Companies," *Adweek*, January

31, 2018, accessed April 2, 2019, https://www.adweek.com/digital/women-minorities-are-still-underrepresented-on-the-boards-of-social-media-and-tech-companies/.

11. "Despite Modest Gains, Women and Minorities See Little Change in Representation on Fortune 500 Boards," Deloitte, February 6, 2017, PR Newswire, https://www.prnewswire.com/news-releases/despite-modest-gains-women-and-minorities-see-little-change-in-representation-on-fortune-500-boards-300402368.html.

12. "Despite Modest Gains, Women and Minorities See Little Change," Deloitte.

13. "Despite Modest Gains, Women and Minorities See Little Change," Deloitte.

14. "Missing Pieces: The 2018 Board Diversity Census of Women and Minorities on Fortune 500 Boards," Alliance for Board Diversity, in collaboration with Deloitte, https://www2.deloitte.com/us/en/pages/center-for-board-effectiveness/articles/missing-pieces-fortune-500-board-diversity-study-2018.html.

15. Author interview, Cyrus Mehri, January 5, 3019.

16. "Missing Pieces Report: The 2016 Board Diversity Census of Women and Minorities on Fortune 500 Boards," Alliance for Board Diversity, in collaboration with Deloitte, https://www2.deloitte.com/us/en/pages/center-for-board-effectiveness/articles/board-diversity-census-missing-pieces.html.

17. Author interview, Lauren Edelman, January 14, 2019.

18. Lauren Edelman, "Legal Ambiguity and Symbolic Structures: Organizational Meditation of Civil Rights Law," *American Journal of Sociology* 97, no. 6 (May 1992): 1531–1576; Lauren B. Edelment, "How HR and Judges Made It Almost impossible for Victims of Sexual Harassment to Win in Court," *Harvard Business Review*, August 22, 2018.

19. Author interview, Lauren Edelman, January 14, 2019.

20. Author interview, Pamela Coukos, December 2018.

21. Author interview, Bari Ellen-Roberts, January 10, 2019.

22. Author interview, Agnes Gund, November 16, 2018.

23. Robin Pogrebin, "MOMA to Close, Then Open Doors to More Expansive View of Art," *New York Times*, February 5, 2019, A1.

24. Author interview, Kirt Von Daacke, December 20, 2018.

25. Author interview, E. Brian Dobbins, November 7, 2018.

26. Author interview, April Reign, January 11, 2019.

27. Darnell Hunt, Ana-Christina Ramón, and Michael Tran, "Hollywood Diversity Report 2019: Old Story, New Beginning," UCLA College of Social Sciences, February 2019, https://socialsciences.ucla.edu/wp-content/uploads/2019/02/UCLA-Hollywood-Diversity-Report-2019-2-21-2019.pdf.

INDEX

Pamela Newkirk is an award-winning journalist and a professor of journalism at New York University who has written extensively about diversity in the news media and art world. She is the author of *Spectacle: The Astonishing Life of Ota Benga*, which won the NAACP Image Award, and *Within the Veil: Black Journalists, White Media*, which won the National Press Club Award for media criticism, as well as the editor of *Letters from Black America*. Newkirk's articles and reviews are regularly published in major media, including the *Washington Post*, the *New York Times*, the *Guardian*, *The Nation*, and the *Chronicle of Higher Education*. She lives in New York City.